Parental Behavior in Diverse Societies

Robert A. LeVine, *Editor*
Harvard University

Patrice M. Miller, *Editor*
Harvard University

Mary Maxwell West, *Editor*
Harvard University

NEW DIRECTIONS FOR CHILD DEVELOPMENT
WILLIAM DAMON, *Editor-in-Chief*
Clark University

Number 40, Summer 1988

Paperback sourcebooks in
The Jossey-Bass Social and Behavioral Sciences Series

Jossey-Bass Inc., Publishers
San Francisco • London

Robert A. LeVine, Patrice M. Miller, Mary Maxwell West (eds.).
Parental Behavior in Diverse Societies.
New Directions for Child Development, no. 40.
San Francisco: Jossey-Bass, 1988.

New Directions for Child Development
William Damon, *Editor-in-Chief*

New Directions for Child Development is published quarterly by
Jossey-Bass Inc., Publishers (publication number USPS 494-090).
Second-class postage paid at San Francisco, California, and at
additional mailing offices. POSTMASTER: Send address changes to
Jossey-Bass Inc., Publishers, 350 Sansome Street, San Francisco,
California 94104.

Editorial correspondence should be sent to the Editor-in-Chief,
William Damon, Department of Psychology, Clark University,
Worcester, Massachusetts 01610.

Library of Congress Catalog Card Number LC 85-644581

International Standard Serial Number ISSN 0195-2269

International Standard Book Number ISBN 1-55542-915-7

Cover art by WILLI BAUM

Manufactured in the United States of America. Printed on acid-free paper.

Ordering Information

The paperback sourcebooks listed below are published quarterly and can be ordered either by subscription or single copy.

Subscriptions cost $52.00 per year for institutions, agencies, and libraries. Individuals can subscribe at the special rate of $39.00 per year *if payment is by personal check*. (Note that the full rate of $52.00 applies if payment is by institutional check, even if the subscription is designated for an individual.) Standing orders are accepted.

Single copies are available at $12.95 when payment accompanies order. (California, New Jersey, New York, and Washington, D.C., residents please include appropriate sales tax.) For billed orders, cost per copy is $12.95 plus postage and handling.

Substantial discounts are offered to organizations and individuals wishing to purchase bulk quantities of Jossey-Bass sourcebooks. Please inquire.

Please note that these prices are for the academic year 1987–88 and are subject to change without notice. Also, some titles may be out of print and therefore not available for sale.

To ensure correct and prompt delivery, all orders must give either the *name of an individual* or an *official purchase order number*. Please submit your order as follows:

Subscriptions: specify series and year subscription is to begin.
Single Copies: specify sourcebook code (such as, CD1) and first two words of title.

Mail orders for United States and Possessions, Australia, New Zealand, Canada, Latin America, and Japan to:
Jossey-Bass Inc., Publishers
350 Sansome Street
San Francisco, California 94104

Mail orders for all other parts of the world to:
Jossey-Bass Limited
28 Banner Street
London EC1Y 8QE

New Directions for Child Development Series
William Damon, *Editor-in-Chief*

CD1   *Social Cognition*, William Damon
CD2   *Moral Development*, William Damon
CD3   *Early Symbolization*, Howard Gardner, Dennie Wolf

Contents

Editors' Notes

Like eagles and elephants, humans take care of their offspring for an extended period after birth. Caretaking arrangements and practices in humans, however, are highly variable from one population to another and even from one generation to another within the same population. Unlike other animals, humans concern themselves with whether their childcare practices make sense in their current lives, and they may change long-standing customs accordingly. They occasionally engage in public discourse over what constitutes good care, who should do it, and what effects it has on children.

The United States is currently engaged in such a public discussion, occasioned by a rapid increase of childbearing women in the labor force and the lack of an established system of care for their children. The question of how children should be cared for when their mothers work raises basic issues concerning the definition and assessment of good care for children at different ages, issues that have been analyzed and investigated in psychological terms (Phillips, 1987). Cross-cultural evidence can contribute to the consideration of these issues by documenting the various ways in which human societies have defined the needs of children and met them under diverse demographic and socioeconomic conditions. By exploring the contexts of parental behavior in other cultures, we uncover universals and variables in the parental predicament and are able to place our current problems in a broader perspective. Thus, this volume proposes a theoretical model and examines its validity in case studies from three continents and in cross-cultural comparisons of mother-infant observations and parental survey data.

The volume originated in a panel on parental goals organized by Mary Maxwell West at the American Anthropological Association meetings in 1982. Colleagues from the Laboratory of Human Development at Harvard were invited to present ethnographic papers based on field research with mothers and children in six societies and to comment on LeVine's (1974) model of parental goals and adaptive behavior. Those papers have become Chapters Two through Seven of this volume. Five of those samples had been studied or analyzed as part of the Comparative Human Infancy Project at Harvard from 1979 to 1982. The comparative analysis of that project's findings appears in Chapter Eight. More recently, Lois W. Hoffman analyzed data from the eight-nation Value of Children study in terms of this adaptive model, and the findings appear in Chapter Nine.

2

We want to thank Martha Zaslow and James Chisholm for their participation on the original panel, and Barbara Talhouni for her assistance in the preparation of this volume. We also want to acknowledge gratefully the support of the Spencer Foundation and the Population Council for much of the research and analysis embodied in this publication.

Robert A. LeVine
Patrice M. Miller
Mary Maxwell West
Editors

References

LeVine, R. A. "Parental Goals: A Cross-Cultural View." *Teachers College Record*, 1974, *76* (2), 226–239.

Phillips, D. (ed.). *Quality in Child Care: What Does Research Tell Us?* Washington, D.C.: National Association for the Education of Young Children, 1987.

Robert A. LeVine is Roy E. Larsen Professor of Education and Human Development at the Harvard Graduate School of Education and professor of anthropology at Harvard University.

Patrice M. Miller is completing her doctoral work at the Harvard Graduate School of Education and is an instructor in psychology at the University of Massachusetts–Boston.

Mary Maxwell West (formerly Katz) is research associate at the Harvard Graduate School of Education where she coordinates research on children's mathematics and science learning.

Parents seek to promote the survival and success of their offspring, but their behavior is adapted to the socioeconomic and demographic conditions of agrarian and urban-industrial societies and further differentiated by local cultural traditions.

Human Parental Care: Universal Goals, Cultural Strategies, Individual Behavior

Robert A. LeVine

In 1974 I formulated a model of parental behavior in terms of adaptation in an article called "Parental Goals: A Cross-Cultural View" (LeVine, 1974). At that time, there seemed to be two theoretical perspectives on human parental care: One, represented by anthropologists such as William Caudill (Caudill and Weinstein, 1969), emphasized the values that parents of different cultures brought to infant care and how those values influenced their observable behavior. The other, represented by the psychiatrist John Bowlby (1969), emphasized infant-caretaker attachment as a universal context constraining variation in parental behavior. The theories and evidence of these perspectives were not necessarily in contradiction, but, as separate approaches to infant care, they contributed to the ongoing opposition between cultural and phylogenetic determinisms. There seemed the need for a model that could encompass universals

The writing of this chapter was supported by the Spencer Foundation.

R. A. LeVine, P. M. Miller, and M. M. West (eds.). *Parental Behavior in Diverse Societies.*
New Directions for Child Development, no. 40. San Francisco: Jossey-Bass, Summer 1988.

4

along with variations, adaptive processes along with cultural imperatives, and actual parental practices along with ideal standards.

Parental Behavior Based on Parental Goals

The existing models had left out the perspectives of the parents themselves in caring for their children. How do parents of a given culture define the requirements of child care during the first years of life, and how do they perceive the obstacles to be overcome in fulfilling these needs? The phylogenetic perspective assumed an innate sensitivity on the part of all mothers (or all human adults) to infant signals for nurturance, but it did not specify the variety of forms of infant care through which this sensitivity was implemented. The cultural perspective assumed that parents were guided by culture-specific models of interpersonal relations—for example, independence would be the model for middle-class Americans, interdependence for middle-class Japanese (Caudill and Weinstein, 1969)—but it did not indicate how these distant goals were integrated with the other aims of parents in a particular culture and with their perceptions of their child's adaptive problems in the early years of life. That parents are influenced by phylogenetic and cultural factors is indisputable, but these influences can only affect children through the activities of parents in a given environmental setting. Parental activity, while constrained by the human genome and directed by cultural values, must also be seen as adjusted, consciously and unconsciously, to those aspects of the environment that threaten or facilitate the attainment of parental goals.

What do parents want? The working model advanced in 1974 proposed a distinction between what parents want *from* their children and what they want *for* their children. The former is more culturally diverse, dividing the largely agrarian societies (in which parents count on their offspring for labor during childhood and for old-age assistance during adulthood) from their largely industrial societies (in which parents rely on their children for neither). Caldwell (1982) provides a specification of this perspective.

What parents want for their children, however, can be conceptualized as universal: survival and health, the acquisition of economic capabilities, and the attainment of whatever other cultural values are locally prevalent. These goals form a rough hierarchical sequence in the course of development, since parents might reasonably want to be assured of infant survival before attending seriously to the child's capabilities for socioeconomic participation, and they might well give priority to the child's future economic security over the development of culturally defined virtues. The goals also constitute framework for adaptation, since local conditions threatening their fulfillment motivate parents to develop strategies for minimizing perceived risks to children and for maximizing their welfare.

This model of parental behavior generated several hypotheses: (1) populations with high infant mortality rates have customs of infant care organized around ensuring infant survival and health, while the pursuit of learning and of behavioral development is postponed until a later age when the child's survival is relatively certain, (2) populations with precarious subsistence resources have customs of child training organized around the acquisition of behavior patterns that will be economically advantageous in adulthood, (3) these customs minimize survival risks under particular local conditions and therefore constitute adaptive patterns, and (4) once they become cultural traditions, these patterns can be (and often are) carried out by parents as tested commonsense formulas that embody a folk wisdom greater than the parents themselves can conceive or explain but which reduces or prevents their anxiety.

This model and its hypotheses represent a cultural evolutionary position in which utilitarian and cultural concepts are combined in a distinctive way. From this viewpoint, humans do not blindly follow a genetic or cultural code in their parental conduct but are rational actors who adjust their behavior to the risks and the benefits they perceive in the environment of child care. As the parents of a given community modify traditional formulas for child care, they help redefine "custom" as adaptive practice rather than arbitrary tradition.

Where environmental risks have been high and stable over many generations, as with infant mortality in sub-Saharan Africa, the customary formulas for infant care become a cultural code that is both adaptive practice and arbitrary tradition—adaptive because it anticipates hazards and provides a practical formula for overcoming them, arbitrary because it is communicated to parents as being the natural, normal, and necessary pathway for parental action rather than a choice among several possibilities. When the situations parents face resemble those of the past, the customary behavior operates to reduce risks in the population; when the situation of environmental risk has changed, the behavior may no longer be adaptive. The question of whether parents will modify the customary formula accordingly depends on the extent to which they can perceive the maladaptive outcome in the child, whether they have the means to adjust their behavior in a more adaptive way, and whether such an adjustment clashes with other influential goals and strategies in their lives.

Though based on assumptions that seem obvious, at least from a utilitarian perspective, the model does not fit into any single framework in the social and biological sciences and represents something of a departure in thinking about parenthood. Some of its hypotheses are testable, providing a challenge to research, and at least one may appear implausible. The notion that folk customs of child care, formulated in the context of local religious and other supernatural beliefs, might act effectively as preventive pediatrics and as household economics may arouse the skepticism of twentieth-century scientists; it certainly requires careful examination in the light of empirical evidence.

In the original article (LeVine, 1974), I used illustrative evidence, mostly from my own fieldwork in Africa, to support the hypotheses. More evidence—confirming, challenging, and elaborating the hypotheses—has become available since 1974 and is presented in this sourcebook. New theoretical perspectives on parental care have also become available, suggesting that the model be recast in terms of the reproductive and socioeconomic characteristics of human populations.

A New Model of Parental Strategies

The analysis of human parental care as adaptive behavior can be expanded to include historical changes in demographic, socioeconomic, and cultural environments. During the last decade, I have offered more inclusive and systematic formulations (LeVine, 1980, 1983, 1984; LeVine and White, 1987), as the study of parental behavior has become an important point of connection between the social and biological sciences (Lancaster, Altmann, Rossi, and Sherrod, 1987). The new model we have developed, in the course of conducting and reflecting on the research reported in this volume, still assumes that all human parents share the goals of survival, economic security, and locally defined virtue for their children, but it also suggests that their cultural codes reflect the opportunities as well as hazards of their historically conditioned environments and represent compromise formulas designed for the accomplishment of multiple goals.

More specifically, our current model is based on the concept of parental investment strategies for allocating time, attention, and domestic resources to the raising of children over the short and long term. Each major type of human socioeconomic adaptation (foraging, agrarian, urban-industrial) is assumed to have an optimal parental investment strategy that reflects its specific incentives and hazards affecting reproduction and that conditions the assumptions with which adults approach parenthood. A parental investment strategy includes an ideal of "quantity" or "quality" in children that guides parents in allocating their resources.

Agrarian Parental Strategies. The optimal parental strategy for agrarian societies, according to this model, is quantitative; it emphasizes high fertility as its primary goal. This reflects the high value of relatively unskilled child labor in domestic food and craft production, the high value of numerous progeny for long-term social support during a parent's later years, the low cost of each child to parents in terms of domestic resources, and the high mortality rate of infants and children. In other words, the demand for children is usually greater than the supply.

The goal of high fertility, however, must be qualified by the obstacles to infant survival in agrarian settings. The largest part of offspring mortality occurs during infancy, and this is increased if children are born too closely together. The goal of agrarian mothers, then, is to maximize the number of *surviving* children by spacing births to prolong the period of exclusive maternal attention, including breast-feeding and cosleeping. This strategy, currently most readily observable in sub-Saharan Africa (Page and Lesthaeghe, 1981), gives each child the best chance at survival while maintaining a regular schedule of births until menopause. The mother gives most attention to each child in turn before it is weaned, particularly in the early months before its survival is regarded as assured; this attention provides physical nurturance and protection during a vulnerable period. Maternal attention in agrarian societies is in the service of folk pediatrics; it is decreased as the child's growth provides confidence of its survival and temporarily increased whenever the child becomes ill.

Urban-Industrial Parental Strategy. The optimal strategy for urban-industrial societies is qualitative; its goals concern the child's acquisition of skills rather than the number of children born. This strategy reflects the fact that children cost more and contribute less in an urban-industrial setting than in an agrarian one; it also reflects low infant and child mortality rates, as well as the pressures of a competitive labor market that operate through an academically graded occupational hierarchy to reward extended (and expensive) preparation for adult roles. The demand for children is accordingly weak compared with agrarian societies, but the supply is kept in balance through contraception and delayed marriage. The task of raising a child is redefined as a voluntary activity demanding much more parental time, energy, and attention over a longer period of time.

In this low-fertility, urban-industrial context, infant care is construed less as nurturance for a child at risk than as mental and social stimulation for a child with a future. Maternal attention is devoted to talking and playing with the baby, creating extended "protoconversations" before the baby is capable of speech and responding to the baby's initiatives for social interaction. As the child gets older, initiates more, and communicates more comprehensibly, the mother increases her attention in response to the child's expectations. Thus, the distribution of maternal attention and effort across the first years of a child's life should be the opposite of that found in agrarian societies; urban-industrial mothers should find themselves committing more attention to their children at two and three than they did at one. We have sometimes called this a high-intensity pattern of care, involving communicative interaction, in contrast with a low-intensity pattern, which seeks primarily to soothe; the former develops increasingly elevated expectations for maternal attention, whereas the latter does not. It must finally be mentioned that the urban-industrial parental investment strategy entails a large commitment not only of parental attention but also of other domestic resources (such as space, furniture, food, clothing, and playthings) to each child over a prolonged period of time.

The empirical validity of this theoretical model is explored in the chapters of this volume. Chapters Two, Three, and Four provide portraits of parental care among agrarian peoples in Fiji, Kenya, and Yucatán, respectively; Chapters Five, Six, and Seven describe urban-industrial parents in Italy, the United States, and Sweden. Chapter Eight compares maternal behavior in the first year of life for five of these peoples, and Chapter Nine compares parental attitudes from national samples of Asian countries and the United States. There is some general support for the model: In Chapter Nine, for example, Hoffman shows that mothers from the most agrarian countries (Indonesia, Philippines, Thailand) mentioned economic utility as a reason for having children much more frequently than mothers from the most urban-industrial ones (Korea, Taiwan, the United States). The research presented in Chapter Eight shows that holding a baby is more frequent among mothers in agrarian countries and that verbal and visual attention to a baby is more characteristic of mothers in urban-industrial ones.

Culture-Specific Influences. The optimal strategies embody general formulas that constrain parental thought about reproduction and child-rearing in a certain type of society, but these formulas do not provide the specific contents of parental attitudes and behavior. Each culture, drawing on its own symbolic traditions, supplies models for parental behavior that, when implemented under local conditions, become culture-specific styles of parental commitment (LeVine and White, 1987, pp. 289–291). It is these patterns of parental activity in local context that affect the health, welfare, and psychological development of children. We must assume that socioeconomic and demographic conditions vary among agrarian societies and among urban-industrial societies and that cultural models for parental behavior will reflect these variations.

Table 1 shows reproductive and educational characteristics of the national populations for which parental patterns are described in the next six chapters. Although the figures for Fiji, Kenya, and Mexico must be regarded as estimates, the table illustrates how conditions that affect parental care may vary within a certain category of society. There is a big gap between the three largely agrarian countries on the left side of the table, which have far higher rates of birth and infant death and much lower rates of female secondary school enrollment, and the three urban-industrial countries on the right. But there are also variations within each category: Kenya, for example, has a much higher birthrate and

Table 1. National Characteristics of Six Countries

	Fiji	Kenya	Mexico	Italy	U.S.	Sweden
Crude birthrate 1984–1985	29	54	33	10	16	11
Infant mortality rate 1984–1985	40	91	50	12	11	6
Infant mortality rate 1955	73	160	83	51	26	17
Female secondary school enrollment (as percentage of age group)	40[a]	16	53	73	95	88

[a] Estimated from Fiji government statistics, 1976.
Source: World Bank, 1987; United Nations, 1985.

infant mortality rate than Fiji and Mexico, suggesting a demographic environment and a level of risk to infants closer to that of the past.

The table also shows, in the second and third rows, major changes in infant mortality for all six of the countries between 1955 and the 1980s. These are indicators of a worldwide improvement in health that has occurred since World War II. Despite the changes everywhere, the range across countries is greater now than it was thirty years ago, as shown by the comparison of Kenya and Sweden then and now, and it should be noted that Kenya has one of the lowest national rates of infant mortality in sub-Saharan Africa. Most noteworthy among the urban-industrial countries is Italy, which had an infant mortality rate in 1955 that was close to those of agrarian populations but that has declined in thirty years to the level of the United States.

These demographic variations are only one of the local forces that shape parental behavior within the constraints of agrarian or urban-industrial parental investment strategies. For example, Chapter Two describes how Fijian mothers, while maintaining a life that is more or less traditional for Pacific Islanders, now deliver their first child in the hospital, use contraception to limit births, and use immunization and medical services to assure child survival. Thus, their birth and infant mortality rates are very low in comparison with other agrarian societies. The domestic economy of Fijians does not seem to rely as heavily on child labor as the agrarian model assumes, nor do they face as severe a threat to infant health and survival. Other research shows that the actual labor contribution of children varies widely among agrarian societies (Nag, White, and Peet, 1978; Munroe, Munroe, and Shimmin, 1984), suggesting that the demand for children as workers might be far from uniform in the agrarian world.

What comes through most clearly in Chapter Two, however, is that Fijians have active traditions of cooperation and reciprocity within domestic groups and local kin networks, so that tasks and resources tend to be shared rather than subject to a limited allocative regime. This means that infant care is not so dependent on the mother's own time-energy budget; it involves other women as well as older children. Mothers breast-feed and sleep with their babies, but the social network for mutual assistance to which mothers and children belong is the primary reality of parenthood. As in other agrarian societies, children are subordinated in the local age hierarchy (for example, they are excluded from the consumption of special foods), but Fijian children are trained primarily to be active participants in a reciprocal social order within which economic sharing and cooperation are assumed. Fijian culture does not simply embody the agrarian parental strategy in a different cultural package; rather, it employs a whole different set of terms for reckoning about adaptation—terms that are characteristic of many Pacific Island cultures, where the adoption of young children and other forms of domestic sharing are more common than elsewhere in the agrarian world.

The Gusii of Kenya, described in Chapter Three, and the Yucatec Mayans of Mexico, described in Chapter Four, raise another set of problems for the agrarian model—namely, the impact of rapid social change on some of its parameters. Both peoples have experienced a sharp drop in infant and child mortality rates, which has enabled them to fulfill traditional fertility goals; meanwhile, a concurrent decline in the average duration of breast-feeding and of birth intervals has increased the number of children born and has created new risks of disease and malnutrition. Gusii mothers are bearing more children than can be fed well, and Mayan mothers are abandoning breast-feeding even though folk belief teaches that it is better for the child's health. This apparently maladaptive behavior occurs in response to the sudden collapse of a long-standing equilibrium. Gusii and Mayan mothers are certainly aware that babies are more likely to survive now than a generation ago, and they seem confident that modern medical care will ensure child survival no matter what else happens. They are right, at least in the short run, in that mortality rates continue to decline while the increasing chronic morbidity and malnutrition are mostly nonlethal during childhood. To these mothers, the survival goal is paramount, and the recent gains over mortality are more salient than losses in the health status of living children. Their guide to adaptive behavior is the modern medical clinic, which is as likely to advise against breast-feeding in Yucatán as it is to be neutral on contraception in southwestern Kenya. The medicalization of child health in both Yucatán and Kenya, with its attention to life-saving medicine and its neglect of the social context of reproduction, has not served these mothers well. Their plight is typical of agrarian societies in demographic transition.

Other examples of variations in parental concepts among agrarian societies can be found in Chapter Nine, where Hoffman shows that, for example, Thailand differs from Indonesia and the Philippines in its lesser emphasis on obedience in the parent-child relationship. This seems to be a function of particular cultural and ideological traditions. Rural parents in these countries are no more frequent in their preference for obedient children than urban ones, but this may be due to the fact that many parents in Third World cities are engaged in domestic production or trade with their children as laborers, just as their country cousins are.

That urban-industrial societies vary as contexts for parental care is equally demonstrable from Chapters Five, Six, and Seven. The differences in standards of care between Italy and the United States are particularly striking and indicate that cultural as well as socioeconomic and demographic factors continue to be influential in differentiating parental behavior.

References

Bowlby, J. *Attachment*. New York: Basic Books, 1969.
Caldwell, J. *Theory of Fertility Decline*. New York: Academic Press, 1982.
Caudill, W., and Weinstein, H. "Maternal Care and Infant Behavior in Japan and America." *Psychiatry*, 1969, *32*, 12–43.
Government of Fiji Bureau of Statistics. *Social Indicators for Fiji*. No. 3. Suva: Government of Fiji Bureau of Statistics, 1976.
Lancaster, J., Altmann, J., Rossi, A., and Sherrod, L. (eds.). *Parenting Across the Life Span*. Hawthorne, N.Y.: Aldine, 1987.
LeVine, R. A. "Parental Goals: A Cross-Cultural View." *Teachers College Record*, 1974, *76* (2), 226–239.
LeVine, R. A. "A Cross-Cultural Perspective on Parenting." In M. Fantini and R. Cardenas (eds.), *Parenting in a Multicultural Society*. New York: Longman, 1980.
LeVine, R. A. "Fertility and Child Development: An Anthropological Approach." In D. A. Wagner (ed.), *Child Development and International Development: Research-Policy Interfaces*. New Directions for Child Development, no. 20. San Francisco: Jossey-Bass, 1983.
LeVine, R. A. *Maternal Behavior and Child Development in High-Fertility Populations*. Fertility Determinants Research Notes, no. 2. New York: The Population Council, 1984.
LeVine, R. A., and White, M. "Parenthood in Social Transformation." In J. Lancaster, J. Altmann, A. Rossi, and L. Sherrod (eds.), *Parenting Across the Life Span*. Hawthorne, N.Y.: Aldine, 1987.
Munroe, R. L., Munroe, R. H., and Shimmin, H. "Children's Work in Four Cultures: Determinants and Consequences." *American Anthropologist*, 1984, *86*, 342–348.
Nag, M., White, B., and Peet, R. "Anthropological Approach to the Study of Economic Value of Children: Java and Nepal." *Current Anthropology*, 1978, *19*, 293–306.
Page, H., and Lesthaeghe, R. (eds.). *Child Spacing in Tropical Africa*. New York: Academic Press, 1981.
United Nations. *United Nations Demographic Yearbook*. New York: United Nations, 1985.
World Bank. *World Development Report, 1987*. New York: Oxford University Press, 1987.

12

Robert A. LeVine is Roy E. Larsen Professor of Education and Human Development at the Harvard Graduate School of Education and professor of anthropology at Harvard University.

Fijian infant care reflects the intertwining of social and economic support characteristic of Fijian rural life; although mothers discontinue subsistence work, the infant is often tended by others, initiating lifelong nurturant relationships.

Parental Values and Behavior in the Outer Fiji Islands

Mary Maxwell West

To interpret parental values and behavior in the outer Fiji Islands as adapted to ensure the basic physical, economic, and social survival of children is, at the broadest level, an easy task. The concerns that parents expressed for their young children's development in 1977–1978 include conscious concern with the infant's physical well-being and with the later development of work skills and social behaviors necessary to their rural farming and fishing life. Actual practices of infant care can also be seen generally as protecting the physical health of infants, and the actual activities of children can be seen to prepare them for adult roles.

On the other hand, one can also find instances of behavior that appear not to serve, or even appear to defeat, children's physical well-

This chapter is partially adapted from M. M. Katz (1984). This study was supported by a grant from the U.S. National Institutes of Mental Health to Beatrice B. Whiting, Harvard Graduate School of Education. I am grateful for this support, as well as to the Fiji Ministries of Health, Education, and Fijian Affairs for permission to conduct research and to use medical records. I also thank Asasela Ravuvu and Ron Crocombe of the Institute of Pacific Studies of the University of the South Pacific for advice; Saiamone Vatu for his support and guidance; Ifereimi Naivota and Sereana Naivota for research assistance and advice; and the parents who participated for their interest and cooperation.

R. A. LeVine, P. M. Miller, and M. M. West (eds.). *Parental Behavior in Diverse Societies.*
New Directions for Child Development, no. 40. San Francisco: Jossey-Bass, Summer 1988.

being or the development of important skills. For example, in Fijian custom, food is served to adult men before it is served to women and children, with the result that young children may receive less of the highly craved protein-rich foods if they are scarce. Health workers concerned about child nutrition in Fiji strove to educate villagers about young children's need for a certain amount of these foods. Similarly, educators questioned whether parents' demands on children for village work diminished children's opportunity to excel in schoolwork and thus their later employability in professional areas. These instances of what seem to be maladaptive practices force us to a much closer analysis of environmental conditions and changes and of culture members' beliefs about them. One conclusion may be that customs appear well adapted to past conditions but not to current ones. If this is the case, we must then ask what psychological mechanisms allow persons to ignore or deny certain aspects of current conditions, and by which mechanisms do customs gain a moral or divine nature that divorces them from the conditions in which they may have originally been adaptive (LeVine and White, 1986).

Another possibility is that we need to reformulate our notion of the constraints on adaptation so that we see them as different, or broader. This chapter is such an exercise, in which practical, individual, and short-term constraints are contrasted with more abstract, social, and long-term ones. Fijian infant care cannot be fully explained in terms of the requirements for infant survival, the nature of the mother's work, the extent of her work load, or the preparation of children for adult work skills. One is forced to take into account the nature of social relationships among those surrounding the infant and the preparation of the infant for these relationships. This goal—the learning of social bonding and sharing—is not stated by parents but is inferred from observations of child and adult life. The sharing of material resources and information that occurs in many domains of daily life—such as in producing and harvesting food, in ceremony, in etiquette, and in leisure—carries a message of social bonding among various kin or lineages. The infant care system serves to initiate the child into, and to reaffirm for the adults, the nurturant relationships among particular kin within the community that continue through adult life in spite of migration. While the economic utility of social bonds in this setting is obvious, the Fijian concept does not separate the economic from the social elements.

The observations reported in this chapter were made in a fifteen-month study of child cognitive development in Kadavu, Fiji, in 1977–1978 (M. M. Katz, 1981). Infants in Nagone village were observed daily, and infants in eight surrounding villages were visited at intervals of two to four months for observations, cognitive testing, and discussions with mothers and other family members.

Setting

The Fiji Islands are located in the southwest Pacific Ocean, approximately 1,300 kilometers (800 miles) east of Vanuatu and the Solomon
Islands, and 1,000 kilometers (620 miles) west of Samoa and Tonga. Australia is 2,740 kilometers (1,700 miles) southwest and New Zealand about
1,770 kilometers (1,100 miles) south. Mean monthly temperature ranges
from twenty-two to twenty-seven degrees centigrade (seventy-one to eighty
degrees Fahrenheit). A Fijian and Fiji-Indian population of over 600,000
clusters in two cities and in towns and villages on two large islands;
numerous outer islands are inhabited by Fijians living in villages of one
hundred to four hundred, practicing farming and fishing, and making
economic exchanges with relatives on the bigger islands.

The families who participated in this study lived in a group of
volcanic islands reached by a six- to twelve-hour journey by boat from
the capital city of Suva. Small cargo or fishing boats and occasionally
larger government boats traveled to and from this area every one to three
weeks, depending on cargo, passengers, and weather. The cost of the trip
was expensive enough to prohibit frequent travel for many families, and
visits to Suva among adults ranged from twice a year to none for several
years. The nine villages surveyed for this study had a total population of
945 and were located on four adjacent islands in an area of about two
hundred square miles, including land and sea. Villages were located on
the coast usually at the mouth of a stream and were usually several miles
apart—an hour or two by foot, less by boat.

The remarkable feature of the physical environment was that food
resources varied considerably from village to village because of variations
in terrain and reefs. Each village had a somewhat distinct eco-niche,
with abundance of some foods and scarcity of others, even though villages
were only a short distance apart. Rain fell unequally on the windward
and leeward sides of the high volcanic mountains, providing forested
and less forested regions and resulting in different types of soil. Fish
resources varied with the varying location and nature of reefs around the
islands. Two small, low islands received less rain than other parts of the
district; the inhabitants of these islands exploited the reefs and ate many
kinds of seafood but had a shortage of vegetables compared with other
villages. The entire district was protected from ocean swells by a distant
barrier reef, creating excellent fishing grounds in relatively protected
waters. Nevertheless, high winds often made boat excursions dangerous
or impossible.

A village consisted of one or two groups of patrilineally related
families totaling 75 to 150 persons. Houses were clustered about seven to
fifteen yards apart in an open area; they were built with reed, timber, or
cement block walls. Wooden floors, or floors raised off the ground by

layers of crushed coral and dried palm leaves, were covered by woven pandanus-leaf mats. In most villages, water was piped into three or four village taps from dammed stream reservoirs high in the hillsides; otherwise, it was caught by house roofs and directed into a central underground cistern. The first road in the area was being built during the time of fieldwork; as yet there were no motor vehicles in the district and travel between villages was by foot or by outboard motorboat.

Garden plots were located outside of the village in the surrounding hillsides, up to an hour's walk away. A field rotation system of agriculture was practiced, with tapioca, taro, and yams being the most common crops. A few vegetables were also cultivated—namely, eggplant, cabbage, a spinachlike vegetable (leaves of Hibiscus manihot Malvaceae), and pumpkin. Coconut trees were abundant, and papayas, bananas, and breadfruit were common. Mangos and oranges were available in some areas as were two varieties of small nut. Barrier and fringing reefs as well as coastal mangrove swamps provided a variety of fish, shellfish, and crabs. In addition, chickens and pigs were raised in all villages.

Except for the few persons employed as teachers or nurses, villagers earned cash from selling, in the distant city of Suva, foods produced through both individual and cooperative labor—mainly copra, fish, yams, and kava. Perhaps because of the difficulty and expense of transport to Suva, however, cash cropping consumed very little of villagers' work effort compared to production for their own use. The fundamental aspects of the economy were found to be similar to those described for Fiji by others: traditional cooperative work and exchanges of goods, both formal and informal (Nayacakalou, 1978; Sahlins, 1962; Thompson, 1949). These mechanisms allowed the particular food resources of one lineage group or village to be spread throughout the village and district and also exchanged between urban and rural areas. Cash was also subject to this kind of distribution; persons earning cash from employment in the towns shared cash and store-bought goods with relatives in the villages through the same formal and informal means.

Adult Work and Education

The daily activities of parents in the study district were very similar; they engaged in farming, fishing, domestic tasks, and communal events. Yet their educational, residential, and employment histories varied (as well as their ages and the size of their families). Younger parents had acquired more schooling, mainly because the number of years of primary school available in the local area had gradually increased during the previous two decades from four years to six or eight years. Secondary schooling was available only in boarding schools, most of which were located near urban areas on the main island. Parental years of schooling varied from four to twelve years and was negatively correlated with age ($r = -0.41$, $n = 49$, $p < 0.01$ for mothers; $r = -0.52$, $n = 33$, $p < 0.01$ for fathers). The mean was seven years of schooling for mothers and fathers.

Due to education and other factors, the extent of past residence in urban areas also varied: 60 percent of mothers and 50 percent of fathers had not lived continuously in an urban area for more than one year, nor had traveled outside Fiji. These parents had been exposed to urban life and values and to the customs of other ethnic groups only in occasional visits to the city or in short-term work there. In other families, parents had attended school on the main islands or had worked there for several years. All villagers learned of national and international events through a Fijian-language radio station. What urban life provided was not simply increased awareness of urban and national life but also actual participation in the urban life-style and close observation of other ethnic groups in the multiethnic environment of the large islands.

Medical Care

The district was served by two nursing stations staffed by one doctor and two nurses. Care of infants was a high priority of the medical stations; the nurse at Nagone was highly responsive to all calls that reached her concerning sick infants. In addition, every infant was immunized for diphtheria, tetanus, typhoid, polio, measles, and smallpox. Sick infants (and adults) were treated with antibiotics.

Marriage and Residence Patterns

Marriages in the study district followed the pattern described for Fiji more generally (Nayacakalou, 1971) in a preference for marriage outside of one's local lineage group and for residence in the husband's village. Sixty-three percent of the married mothers were from a village other than the one in which they currently resided: Thirty-seven percent were from a neighboring village (on the same or a nearby island), and 26 percent were from a distant village. Marriages between neighboring villages were especially important because, in the Fijian kinship system, marriage bonds provide channels of political and material support (Becker, 1983; Nayacakalou, 1978; Sahlins, 1962; Thompson, 1949). Because natural resources varied noticeably between villages, the informal exchanges of goods that occurred between persons related by marriage and living in neighboring villages were clearly advantageous. These relatives visited each other frequently, perhaps one to four times a month, and visits were happy occasions with a distinct etiquette. Visitors brought food gifts with them, were welcomed with hearty meals and with social ceremonial drinking (of kava) in the village, and given food gifts on departure. More formal ceremonies accompanying life-cycle events also reaffirmed the bonds between relatives and included much larger exchanges of goods. These ceremonies had a standard form: Two groups of people are defined, quantities of goods and food are presented, and formal speeches stress the identity of each group and their coming together as one, followed by feasting and dancing.

Infant Births and Mortality

Menarche was reported to occur in girls between fourteen and seventeen years of age, and the mean age at first childbirth (of mothers whose first child had been born within the previous ten years) was 20.9 years ($n = 31$, range = 17 to 28 years, SD = 2.5 years). The medical department recommended that first births and those later than fifth be delivered in the hospital in Suva, and most mothers followed this practice. They traveled to Suva in late pregnancy and stayed there for a few months. Mothers could also undergo tubal ligation in Suva if they wished. Otherwise, births occurred in the local clinic or village, usually attended by a nurse or doctor or, if transport could not be arranged, by midwives. Even if the nurse was not able to attend the birth due to difficulty of transport, she examined the infant within a day or two. The interval between recent births (calculated from medical records of birthdates for those who had more than one child under the age of six years) ranged from fifteen to thirty-six months, averaging 25.3 months ($n = 39$, SD = 5.6 months).

The infant mortality rate for Fiji was reported in 1974 as forty deaths per 1,000 infants in the first year of life, twenty-four per 1,000 in the second year, and eight per 1,000 in the third (Government of Fiji Bureau of Statistics, 1976). Twenty years earlier, the same source reports the mortality rate in the first year as seventy-three deaths per 1,000 infants. There were no deaths among the seventy-seven infants in the study sample (born in the years 1975–1977) during the fifteen months of the fieldwork, nor were any deaths of younger infants reported. Thus, the general picture is one of good infant and maternal health, of significant improvement within the past generation, and of local medical help for illnesses but not for serious accidents.

Cultural Values and Infant Care

Importance of Sharing. Sharing is supported in the etiquette of everyday interaction in economic exchanges, as well as in other exchanges that are not obviously of economic benefit. The woman whose net draws plenty of fish shares with another not so lucky or with one who did not go fishing that day. When people visit between households or villages, gifts of food are exchanged. When eating at home, one calls out to anyone passing by, *"Mai kana"* ("come and eat"). The most salient form of social bonding and sharing lies in the ceremonial life. However, the importance of sharing and social togetherness appear to extend beyond strictly practical or immediate economic aspects, since both work and leisure occur by preference in groups. Indeed, the socially withdrawn person is said to be "thinking too much," and a person who is habitually unsocial is regarded with suspicion of witchcraft.

The following traits were most frequently mentioned by adults asked to describe "ideal" Fijian character (R. Katz, 1981): respect for traditions, customs, and other persons; togetherness and group solidarity; good-naturedness and kind-heartedness; and generosity to all. Similar values were noted five years earlier by Hickson (1975) in another part of Fiji. Thus, the conception of ideal character verbalized by adults also stress group membership and responsible social behavior.

Values for Infants. What values pertain specifically to the infancy period? Mothers' verbally expressed values and goals for their one- to three-year-old children are revealed in their answers to several informal interview questions: Does Jone sometimes do things that are wrong? Does Jone sometimes do something that makes you feel happy or proud? Should parents teach some things to children of this age, and what?

The 330 items mentioned by the forty mothers interviewed cluster around the three general values that are consistent with the portrait of parental goals in agrarian societies drawn by LeVine (1974; LeVine and White, 1986) and with earlier discussions of the socialization of respect and obedience among agricultural peoples (Whiting and Whiting, 1975). These values are: respecting property and other rules of proper behavior (25 percent of the items); learning of the service role (21 percent of the items); not doing things that would endanger health, such as running around, leading to falling, or becoming chilled, leading to illness (7 percent of the items). In answer to the second question, a fourth unrelated value emerged—amusing the parent with dancing or singing (15 percent of the items). This response is interesting in that the Fijian word for "happy" (*marau*) also refers to traditional singing and dancing. In fact, mothers often did encourage their young children in dancing movements almost as soon as they could stand up, and they usually would ask them to perform for visitors in the house.

Concern for Infant Health. Infant health was also the focus of strong beliefs about maternal care, nursing, and birth spacing. The nursing mother should not go out fishing, which requires walking deeply into cold water, because the milk will become bad. Nor should she leave the infant to go for long treks out of the village. The infant should be nursed until able to walk well or preferably to run. If a nursing mother becomes pregnant, the child can develop a disease called *save* in which the legs become weak and the child does not eat well. Another disease can befall the mother if intercourse begins too soon after childbirth.

Multiple regression analyses (Katz, 1984) show that birth interval decreased with the amount of education the father had and increased where the mother had relatives in a nearby village. Villagers blamed violation of customary postpartum abstinence (for the duration of breast-feeding) mainly on the father; it may be that greater education, also related to life in urban areas, led fathers to have less respect for this custom. On the other hand, where the mother's kin lived in a neighboring village, the father would experience more shame in violating this strong cultural value. Similarly, duration of breast-feeding increased if mother's kin lived in a neighboring village and decreased among young and more educated fathers. In addition, duration of breast-feeding decreased if mother's kin lived in the same village because such mothers were likely to have a more reliable food supply for the family, including the infant. These correlations indicate the significant effects of the nature and extent of kin bonds, with their intertwined economic and social aspects, on the infant care system.

Importance of Procreativity. The concern for infant health accompanies a strong value on procreativity. Judging from the number of children of several mothers who had chosen to undergo tubal ligation, ideal family size would be five to eight children. The value of children was not merely to provide additional help with subsistence work, but having children fulfilled an ideal of procreativity associated with carrying on the ancestral line. Until bearing children, a married woman was not clearly in the category of the adult woman but was in an ambiguous status more like the unmarried young woman. The principal achievement of adulthood, bearing children, ensured the continuance of the lineage and created new links in the social matrix, which would expand again when each child married. These links add to the family's social status and psychological well-being as well as to their material well-being.

Women's Work and Infant Care. Adult women's work was culturally defined to include providing the green vegetable or seafood portion of the daily meal; preparing, serving, and cleaning up after meals; gathering firewood and coconuts; washing clothes and carrying water from the tap; weaving mats; and making oil (used to oil the skin). Mats and oil were important goods presented in large quantities to other groups on ceremonial occasions. The food resources that women provided were an important part of the diet and were perhaps even more essential in the past when canned fish was not available.

Some of a woman's necessary food-providing work was incompatible with carrying an infant (Brown, 1970; Whiting, 1981). In fishing, women waded or dove into the water; even shallow-water activities would have caused an infant being carried to become wet and chilled. Although plant- and firewood-gathering as well as some domestic work could perhaps be done while carrying an infant in a sling, this did not occur.

Infants were tied to the back with a piece of cloth only when the baby was fussy or when the mother walked between villages.

The availability of social resources in Fijian culture allowed the mother to be excused from work and to be near the infant continuously, facilitating breast-feeding. The foods that the mother would typically provide were provided instead by other women or by her husband, compensating for the mother's decreased foraging. A similar system of material and social support for mothers is described by Thompson (1940) for another outer island during the 1930s, and infant care in several other Pacific cultures where women engage in fishing follows the same pattern (Obrist, 1983; Barlow, 1985; Carrier, 1985).

Shared Infant Care. Although Fijian nursing mothers were thus able to remain near their infants, these mothers still received considerable help with infant care from both children and adults. While mothers usually bathed and dressed infants themselves, others often held, watched over, or engaged in playful social interactions with infants.

Table 1 shows distribution of caregiving observed at three age periods for the thirteen preschool children in Nagone village. Although the mother was present in 70 percent of observations of unweaned infants (ranging in age from seven to twelve months) and in 60 percent of observations of weaned infants (aged thirteen to fifty months), she was the caregiver (actually giving care or the only one available to do so) in half or less at all age points. Someone other than the mother was holding or touching the infant in 30 percent of observations at seven to twenty months. The mean number of other persons in the immediate environment of infants was four. The only time that infants were alone was when they were sleeping, and then an adult was always within hearing distance.

When mothers were asked about who helps them care for young children, they mentioned grandmothers, adolescent and school-age girls, their sisters, and sometimes their husbands. In Nagone village the second most frequent caregivers were adolescent or school-age girls.

The allocation of care and attention can be explained utilizing two different assumptions: First, infant care is a chore; second, infants are persons with specific culturally defined relationships to others. On the one hand, watching an infant was a simple chore that the mother could delegate to her juniors. On the other hand, attention and nurturance were culturally prescribed aspects of certain kin relationships— for example, between grandfather and first grandson, between mother's younger brother and her male child, between father's sister and his female child, and between the child and the child's namesake. The social attention paid to an infant by various relatives, both male and female, constituted a form of culturally prescribed help with infant care.

The nature of the infant's relationship with the mother and with others was different. Lively playful interactions with infants were more

Table 1. Early Social Environment and Care in Nagone Village: Percent of Daytime Hours

	Age in months[a]		
	7–12	13–20	38–50
1. *n*	6	6	6
2. Observations per child	12–15	17–22	10–14
3. Total observations	87	103	71
4. Sleeping	17	12	3
5. Nonmaternal caretakers	46	53	50
6. Mother clearly in charge or caretaking	51	39	27
7. Several possible caretakers, none actively caretaking	0	13	33
Awake Only			
8a. Physical contact with *someone*	56	43	13
8b. Physical contact with mother	27	11	1.4
9. No one within one meter	18	31	43
10. Mother present in immediate sphere	69	62	60
11. Father present in immediate sphere	18	18	19
	(*n* = 5)	(*n* = 5)	(*n* = 4)

[a]There was only one two-year-old child in the village, so data for this age point are unavailable.

Source: Katz, 1984.

characteristic of nonparental interactions than parental. While mothers performed routine physical care of infants, they might engage occasionally in playful interactions with them. But the playful interactions of the nonmaternal caregivers in the household or of relatives visiting from other households were much more notable. Various persons, of all ages and either sex, greeted infants enthusiastically and often initiated playful slaps or clapping games, or engaged the infant in reciprocal vocal or (later) verbal routines. These more highly dramatized routines may have functioned to introduce infants to the significant others in the social matrix, as well as to confirm among adults that the caregiver felt the appropriate concern for the infant, given their particular relationships.

The pattern of physical contact shows that the infant quickly became physically independent of the mother while also experiencing contact with others. While unweaned infants (seven to twelve months) were in physical contact with some person in 56 percent of observations, only half of that was with the mother. At thirteen to twenty months among weaned infants, physical contact was only slightly lower (43 percent), and only one-quarter was with the mother. At age three years, it was 13 percent, and the proportion of maternal contact was one-tenth. As has been documented for most settings other than the urban-industrial ones, infants slept with the mother until weaning or until replaced by another infant, and then slept with another member of the household throughout early childhood.

Examination of the kind of work that was occurring during the observations provides further evidence that the allocation of caregiving served purposes other than merely enabling the mother to perform necessary chores. As indicated, when the mother was near the infant, she was not always the person taking care of it. But the task she pursued was often one that could have been performed appropriately and equally well by the person who was caring for the infant at the moment. For example, the mother might be peeling tapioca while an adolescent girl played with the infant. In other observations, the observed caretaker was a male, a higher status female, or a guest, who could not appropriately have performed the mother's task. In most of these cases, however, there was no reason of health or safety for the infant to be held; the child would have been safe either lying on the mat or toddling around the house. Thus, infant holding and social interactions in this setting appear to have a degree of social function, rather than deriving only from the practical needs of mother's work or of infant health and safety.

Conclusion

My interpretation of this infant care pattern as having important social functions is consistent with interpretations that anthropologists have made in several other Pacific societies: Martini and Kirkpatrick's (1981) study of early interaction in the Marquesas; the discussions of Firth (1963 [1936]), Carroll (1970), Levy (1970), and Rubenstein (1978) on the function of adoption in downplaying bonds in the immediate biological family and dramatizing other relationships; and Ochs's (1982) and Gegeo and Watson-Gegeo's (1985) discussion of ways young children are taught to decenter.

The extent to which the cultural value on social connectedness in Fiji operates loosely from, or in delayed or immediate response to, economic factors could not be shown without longitudinal data. But even some association found between these factors would not dismiss the interesting intertwining of the social and economic that are a part of the Fijian conception of the situation. This is well summarized in a statement of the Fijian anthropologist Rusiate Nayacakalou (1978) about Fijian economic and social life: "The important thing is not that Fijian exchange is not trade, but that the framework within which it takes place is primarily social, not economic. The economic relationship is brought about because of the social relationship; the economic need is solved through a social mechanism; the economic transaction gives expression to an existing social relationship, part of whose function is to satisfy this type of need" (p. 40).

References

Barlow, K. "The Social Context of Infant Feeding in the Murik Lakes of Papua New Guinea." In L. Marshall (ed.), *Infant Care and Feeding in the South Pacific.* New York: Gordon and Breach, 1985.

Becker, A. "Women's Group Formation and Maintenance in Rural Western Fiji." Unpublished senior thesis, Harvard University, 1983.

Brown, J. K. "A Note on the Division of Labor." *American Anthropologist,* 1970, 72, 1073–1078.

Carrier, A. H. "Infant Care and Family Relations on Ponam Island, Papua New Guinea." In L. Marshall (ed.), *Infant Care and Feeding in the South Pacific.* New York: Gordon and Breach, 1985.

Carroll, V. "What Does Adoption Mean?" In V. Carroll (ed.), *Adoption in Eastern Oceania.* Honolulu: University of Hawaii Press, 1970.

Firth, R. *We, the Tikopia: Kinship in Primitive Polynesia.* Boston: Beacon Press, 1963. (Originally published 1936.)

Gegeo, D., and Watson-Gegeo, K. "Kwara'ae Mothers and Infants: Changing Family Patterns in Health, Work, and Childrearing." In L. Marshall (ed.), *Infant Care and Feeding in the South Pacific.* New York: Gordon and Breach, 1985.

Government of Fiji Bureau of Statistics. *Social Indicators for Fiji.* No. 3. Suva: Government of Fiji Bureau of Statistics, 1976.

Hickson, L. "The Isoro: Social and Psychological Factors of Dispute Settlement and Punishment Avoidance in Fiji." Unpublished doctoral dissertation, Harvard University, 1975.

Katz, M. M. "Gaining Sense in the Outer Fiji Islands: A Cross-Cultural Study of Cognitive Development." Unpublished doctoral dissertation, Harvard Graduate School of Education, 1981.

Katz, M. M. "Infant Care in a Group of Outer Fiji Islands." *Ecology of Food and Nutrition,* 1984, 15 (4), 323–340.

Katz, R. "Education as Transformation: Becoming a Healer Among the Kung and the Fijians." *Harvard Educational Review,* 1981, 51 (1), 57–78.

LeVine, R. A. "Parental Goals: A Cross-Cultural View." *Teachers College Record,* 1974, 76 (2), 226–239.

LeVine, R. A., and White, M. I. *Human Conditions: The Cultural Basis of Educational Development.* London: Routledge & Kegan Paul, 1986.

Levy, R. "Tahitian Adoption as a Psychological Message." In V. Carroll, (ed.), *Adoption in Eastern Oceania.* Honolulu: University of Hawaii Press, 1970.

Martini, M., and Kirkpatrick, J. "Early Interactions in the Marquesas Islands." In T. Field, A. M. Sostek, P. Vietze, and P. H. Leiderman (eds.), *Culture and Early Interactions.* Hillsdale, N.J.: Erlbaum, 1981.

Nayacakalou, R. R. "The Fijian System of Kinship and Marriage." In A. Howard (ed.), *Polynesia: Readings on a Culture Area.* Scranton, Penn.: Chandler, 1971.

Nayacakalou, R. R. *Tradition and Change in the Fijian Village.* Suva, Fiji: South Pacific Social Sciences Association, Institute of Pacific Studies, University of the South Pacific, 1978.

Obrist, B. "The Study of Infant Feeding: Suggestions for Further Research." Paper presented at the 12th annual meeting of the Association for Social Anthropology, Oceania, New Harmony, Indiana, Feb. 1983.

Ochs, E. "Talking to Children in Western Samoa." *Language in Society,* 1982, 11 (1), 77–104.

Rubenstein, D. "Adoption on Fais Island: An Ethnography of Childhood." Paper presented at the annual meetings of the American Anthropological Association, Los Angeles, Dec. 1978.

Sahlins, M. *Moala*. Ann Arbor: University of Michigan Press, 1962.

Thompson, L. *Southern Lau: An Ethnography*. Bulletin no. 162. Honolulu: Bernice P. Bishop Museum, 1940.

Thompson, L. "The Relations of Men, Animals, and Plants in an Island Community (Fiji)." *American Anthropologist*, 1949, *51*, 253–267.

Whiting, B. B., and Whiting, J.W.M. *Children of Six Cultures*. Cambridge, Mass.: Harvard University Press, 1975.

Whiting, J.W.M. "Environmental Constraints on Infant Care Practices." In R. H. Munroe, R. L. Munroe, and B. B. Whiting (eds.), *Handbook of Cross-Cultural Human Development*. New York: Garland, 1981.

Mary Maxwell West (formerly Katz) is research associate at the Harvard Graduate School of Education where she coordinates research on children's mathematics and science learning.

Gusii patterns of reproduction and child care evolved in an agrarian setting in which land was abundant and children were scarce. With land now scarce and children abundant, parents continue to be resourceful and strategic in their infant care, but they have not altered their reproductive goals.

Parental Strategies Among the Gusii of Kenya

Robert A. LeVine, Sarah E. LeVine

The Gusii are an agrarian people with a population of about one million, characterized by high fertility and infant mortality rates, who inhabit the highlands of southwestern Kenya east of Lake Victoria. This chapter asks whether their goals and strategies as parents can be seen as adaptive or maladaptive, and in what ways. Three more specific questions help to organize our discussion: To what extent can we explain Gusii cultural traditions of reproduction and parental care in terms of a plausible model of adaptation? To what extent are the observable practices of Gusii parents efficacious—that is, do they have adaptive or maladaptive outcomes for the child? Are the customs and practices of Gusii parents changing in (adaptive) response to changes in their socioeconomic environment?

Adaptive Strategies of the Precolonial Gusii

The precolonial Gusii lived by subsistence agriculture and animal husbandry organized on a domestic basis; each residential family raised

Fieldwork during 1974–1976 was supported by the National Science Foundation and the National Institute of Mental Health; analyses of data were supported by the Spencer Foundation and the Population Council.

R. A. LeVine, P. M. Miller, and M. M. West (eds.). *Parental Behavior in Diverse Societies.*
New Directions for Child Development, no. 40. San Francisco: Jossey-Bass, Summer 1988.

its own food. Like other peoples of the East African highlands, they cultivated an extremely fertile soil with a labor-intensive technology based on the short-handled hoe. Land was abundant until well into this century; shifting cultivation of African millets and (later) maize was practiced, along with the raising of cattle, sheep, and goats. Settlements were partly migratory, since there was a continual demand for new fields and pastures as the population expanded and as internal conflict created emigration.

Before their conquest by the British in 1908, and even after it until well into the 1930s, the Gusii were a frontier people, moving to new localities with their spears, hoes, animals, and a minimum of other baggage. Arts and crafts were not highly developed, market trade was nonexistent, and, prior to British administration, there was no central government. Gusii activities were largely organized to produce food and to protect their settlements and cattle from raids by other Gusii clans and by surrounding peoples. The other primary goal of social life was reproduction, including courtship, marriage, and the rearing of children. Marriage was problematic, because each Gusii settlement consisted of a patrilineal-descent group that recognized a rule of clan exogamy and had to recruit its wives from neighboring clans regarded as potential enemies. Thus, a great deal of energy went into the intergroup transactions and rituals that made marriage and childbearing possible.

Fertility Needs. It is hard to exaggerate the importance of humans as resources for precolonial Gusii. Each domestic group, consisting of a man, his wives, and his children, lived on its own land with its own domestic animals and worked as a team to produce and process food. Men built the houses, broke ground, and planted millet; with their neighboring kinsmen, they herded and milked cattle and acted as a local militia to defend the cows and the young women from the warriors of other clans. Women did the routine cultivation, processed crops, cooked the food, and were responsible for the care of children. Children carried water, herded sheep and goats, provided daytime care for infants, and fetched and carried for their mothers; as they approached puberty, children also helped with cultivating the crops. In the age hierarchy of the homestead, it was as important to have children to whom tasks could be delegated as it was to have women who managed them. As they grew up, sons added to the cattle-herding militia, and daughters were married off to men in other clans, bringing the family bridewealth cattle that expanded the herd and that were used for the marriages of men in the family. Thus, each man, woman, and child was considered a valuable resource.

The amount of land a man could control in precolonial Gusiiland was limited only by the number of wives he had to cultivate it and the number of sons he had to defend it. Men sought more wives, and through them, more land, children, and cattle for personal enrichment, prestige, and power. Wives and cattle expanded food resources in the short run and reproductive resources in the long run. Since land was abundant, wives and children, like cattle, represented self-reproducing assets to be proliferated if possible throughout the husband's life.

Following this formula for economic and demographic expansion, the Gusii population grew and covered an increasing area, producing surplus food as well as cash crops for export after World War II. Their expansion as industrious agriculturalists constitutes fulfillment of the adaptive goals—namely, production and reproduction—that the Gusii share with other agrarian peoples; it also represents a success story they cannot forget. The logic of their indigenous formula for domestic growth remains influential in the thinking of Gusii parents, despite a change in one of its basic conditions—the availability of land. Once all the land had been claimed, cattle and humans began to represent costs as well as assets. Families reduced their herds to the vanishing point but continued to bear children. Sons divided up the land they inherited into smaller and smaller parcels, as population density surpassed 1,000 per square mile in many parts of Gusiiland. A successful formula for growth does not necessarily work when a steady state has been reached.

Population Growth and Land Scarcity. In 1979, the average Gusii woman forty to forty-five years of age had 8.7 live births, making the Gusii one of the most fertile of contemporary human populations, and, although the infant mortality rate was still high (about eighty per 1,000 live births), it had been halved in thirty years and was descending rapidly. The annual growth rate of the Gusii population was more than 4 percent, a rate that means the population will double every seventeen years. Even though additional lands for Gusii settlement have been opened up in the last twenty-five years, and many Gusii have attended schools and taken jobs in the city, the scale of their demographic expansion guarantees that there will be scarcity and even hardship.

Gusii population growth can be understood as the outcome of a reproductive pattern that was adaptive so long as land was abundant and child mortality high. Under those conditions, the high fertility of Gusii women was a reproductive accomplishment that did not threaten a balanced ratio of people to resources. When one out of five or six babies was dying in the first year of life and there was a great demand for domestic labor to work the land, the most urgent adaptive goal was to maximize the number of surviving offspring. This was accomplished through a social organization (including polygyny, bridewealth transactions, and widow reassignment) that placed every woman in a reproductive union and ensured her giving birth regularly from marriage to menopause, while at the same time maintaining a birth interval of well over two years to reduce the risks to infant survival.

30

In this context, Gusii mothers were concerned not only to bear as many children as possible but also to do as much as possible for the growth and survival of each one during the most vulnerable early period. The customary formula for survival was intensive breast-feeding, maternal cosleeping at night and maximum availability consistent with work obligations during the daytime, continuous holding (by a child nurse if the mother was working in the fields), responsiveness to crying, sensitivity to signs of distress and disease—and, most important of all, not getting pregnant again too early. This apparently worked to keep infant and child mortality within bounds, despite the lack of modern medical services, while fertility was rising.

The rise in fertility probably began because of a drop in the age at marriage early in the colonial period, and was later augmented by the economic changes that made polygyny too expensive for younger husbands, which resulted in a shortening of the birth interval as more reproductive unions were monogamous. When infant and child mortality fell after the 1950s, Gusii mothers seem to have become more confident about each child's chances of survival and less concerned about maintaining as long a birth interval as their mothers did. Beginning their reproductive lives earlier and spacing births more closely together, Gusii women became as fertile as any on earth—and increasingly saw the vast majority of their offspring survive. Thus, Gusii customs of reproductive and infant care were highly adaptive in an environment of abundant land, an agrarian economy, and high offspring mortality, but became increasingly maladaptive once those environmental parameters had fundamentally changed.

The current outcomes of retaining these Gusii parenting customs in the face of two or three generations of change include overcrowded land, an increasing number of impoverished rural families, and the menace of child malnutrition. One reason why Gusii parents have not changed more rapidly to a small-family ideal is that they are imbued with confidence that economic opportunities will continue to proliferate in the future. Their confidence is based on traditional models of abundance rather than on a reasoned analysis of the opportunity structure in contemporary Kenya. While the situation of the rural Gusii seems bleak, their adaptive resources have not been exhausted, and the outcome of their struggle for survival is not yet clear.

Maternal Care and Infant Outcomes

How effective are the observable practices of Gusii mothers in responding to the hazards that threaten survival, health, and other goals during infancy? This is one of the questions investigated in the longitudinal study we conducted among the Gusii from 1974 to 1976 (LeVine and others, forthcoming). That Gusii mothers were effective during that time is suggested by the fact that the proportion of children in Kisii District who died within two years of birth, reported by mothers twenty to twenty-four years of age, declined from 12.7 percent in the 1969 national census to 9.8 percent in 1979—almost a 25 percent reduction in a decade. While the change may be partly attributable to the increasing availability of such resources as family income and maternal schooling (Moseley, 1983) that influence preventive and curative health care in the district, it indicates that the larger population of Gusii young mothers from which our sample was drawn in 1975 was acting on behalf of the survival of their children, using whatever old and new resources were available—as we independently discovered when we opened a pediatric clinic that was soon besieged by mothers with babies and young children.

Our study found that Gusii mothers concentrated more of their attention on the period in which they consider the infant most vulnerable (namely the first year and particularly the early months); that they responded with sensitivity to folk indicators of risk in the growth and development of the child; and that they sought to produce a manageable and quiet baby. These practices were effective in responding to the survival risks of the first year of life and seem to be effective in maximizing survival chances altogether, but they can put the child at risk for malnutrition and other developmental problems during the second year. The following subsections give some highlights from our findings.

Healthy Babies. The mothers in our longitudinal samples gave birth to large, healthy, full-term babies. Neonatal assessment showed them to be well organized behaviorally and superior in their motor maturity (Dixon, Keefer, Tronick, and Brazelton, 1982). Their growth in height and weight was excellent during the first six months but thereafter fell below international norms and remained there during the second year. Similarly, their scores on the Bayley Mental Development Index were high during the first year but fell thereafter and remained at a lower level during the second year of life. The overall picture is consistent with the notion that environmental support for infant health and growth is strong during pregnancy and in the postpartum period but becomes weaker over the course of the first year and during the second.

Intensive Care for Vulnerable Infants. Mothers provided more protective attention in the early months of life for those infants who showed signs of being vulnerable. Those infants who were rated as not well organized (poor habituation and motor performance) on the Brazelton Neonatal Behavioral Assessment Scale were held more by their mothers and received more intense maternal response to their crying during the first three months. Babies who weighed less during the first nine months were held more by mother and other caregivers combined (Caron, 1985). Mothers tended to use infant size and motor milestones as intuitive indicators of health, diminishing their attentive care to those who seemed to be progressing well and prolonging such care for those who were slower. These folk practices are responsive to individual differences in gross aspects of infant development and appear well designed for child survival goals.

Quiet, Docile Children. Rapid responsiveness to infant crying resulted in much less infant crying among the Gusii babies at three to four months than in a comparable U.S. sample, as shown in Chapter Eight. Gusii practices of soothing, then, produce quiet and easily managed babies, something desired by Gusii mothers so that they can use child nurses for infant care with minimal trouble and so that the infant will become a more docile toddler who can easily tolerate replacement in the mother's attention when the next child is born. This must also count as effectiveness in infant care, at least by Gusii criteria.

Gusii maternal care during infancy thus involves adaptive rather than routine expertise (Hatano and Inagaki, 1985), since Gusii mothers, rather than rigidly following a customary code, are responsive to differentials in infant characteristics over time and across individuals, even though most cannot formulate the general rules for such distributions. The Gusii strategy of infant care also makes adaptive sense within the context of high fertility goals, fairly high infant mortality rates, and the heavy work load of Gusii mothers, however far it might be from optimal conditions for child development in general.

Parental Responses to Historical Change

Have Gusii parents altered their practices in response to environmental changes over the last few decades, and, if so, has their response been adaptive in terms of the survival, health, and economic capacities of children? As we see it, in every way except fertility, Gusii parents are very sensitive and responsive to new opportunities and problems in child care. An obvious example is infant feeding. In the 1950s, when Gusii mothers returned to the work of cultivation after childbirth, they were supposed by custom to instruct the child nurse to force-feed the crying infant millet gruel from a calabash by blocking the baby's nostrils so that it would aspirate the gruel—a risky and wasteful way of feeding, but one that gets food into the stomach. Even then, younger mothers were giving up the practice (LeVine and LeVine, 1966, p. 123). By 1974, when plastic bottles with rubber nipples had become available, all mothers used them to feed gruel as well as cow's milk, and the custom of force-feeding was virtually unknown. Thus, a risky way of administering food supplements in the first year of life was replaced by a safer way, or, perhaps more accurately, a way in which the risks were hidden rather than visible.

There was also a decline in the duration of breast-feeding, reflecting the decline in polygyny (among other factors), but the average Gusii infant was still being breast-fed until about seventeen months and was thus receiving maximum benefit from the nutrient and protective qualities of breast milk. The contraction of the birth interval augmented fertility, but its risks to health were reduced by the greater availability of health services and the cash income necessary to use them. Although any decline in the duration of breast-feeding and abbreviation of the birth interval can be seen as endangering the child, most of the Gusii mothers observed in the 1970s were mitigating this potential hazard in their reproductive and health-seeking behavior.

A less visible change in custom concerned birth ceremonies. Older mothers in the 1950s reported having performed a series of ceremonies shortly after the birth of each child designed to protect and safeguard the infant; these were no longer practiced in the community by 1956 but were probably going on in the surrounding area. By 1974, however, the same ceremonies were performed only for infants believed to be at great risk, such as twins and those delivered prematurely or with a breech presentation. We interpret this change as reflecting a general diminution of concern for the survival of each child during the period when the infant mortality rate was dropping precipitously. Up to the time of World War II, every child born was considered to be at risk for survival, and with good reason, considering an infant mortality rate that might have been close to 200 per 1,000 live births. As the infant mortality rate was brought down by disease control and the reduction of other environmental risks to child health, parents gained confidence that each child would live and relaxed the intense, public concern embodied in birth ceremonies, which were preserved for cases of extreme risk. If this interpretation is valid, it shows a responsiveness of customary practice to the demographic realities faced by Gusii parents.

Finally, it must be mentioned that by 1974 Gusii parents were sending their children to primary school and mobilizing resources to enable those who gained entry to secondary school and even university to take advantage of what were now considered the most important economic opportunities. This meant less child labor and less parental control in general over their own children, but parents were willing to sacrifice this in the short run for the long-run benefits of children with jobs and income. Despite the population growth and the sluggish economy, Gusii parents had strategies for their own offspring, such as assigning the first-born son to leave school as soon as he was qualified to get a job, so that his wages could pay for the school fees of younger sons who would be permitted to go as far as their academic achievements would take them. In similar fashion, Gusii men of means continued to take additional wives but sometimes kept only one at home working the fields

34

while another managed a shop in the town. Rather than giving up the goals of high fertility and polygyny, then, Gusii tended to adapt these traditional forms of family life to the new economic realities of educational and commercial development. This is clearly adaptive, but it is equally clear that in an environment of economic scarcity, not everyone can win at this game. Thus, the long-term result of Gusii adaptation is an increasing division between rich and poor families, representing upward and downward spirals of socioeconomic mobility.

Conclusion

This brief review has proposed that the Gusii were well adapted, in their customs of reproduction and parental care, to the precolonial environment of southwestern Kenya; that their practices of infant care were effective for child survival during the mid 1970s; and that their parental strategies respond adaptively to a changing structure of demographic pressures and economic opportunities. We have also pointed out that the parental strategies of the Gusii are predicated on the goal of high fertility, which was once a means of economic advancement but is now the greatest threat to economic well-being. And, while the evidence suggests that the adaptiveness of the Gusii will eventuate in their curtailing fertility, the big question is how far environmental degradation, poverty, and malnutrition will have advanced before population growth is brought under control.

References

Caron, J. "Infant Effects on Caretaker Responsiveness: Influences of Infant Characteristics on the Infant Care Environment Among the Gusii of Kenya." Unpublished doctoral thesis, Harvard Graduate School of Education, 1985.
Dixon, S., Keefer, C., Tronick, E., and Brazelton, T. B. "Perinatal Circumstances and Newborn Outcome Among the Gusii of Kenya: Assessment of Risk." *Infant Behavior and Development,* 1982, *5,* 11–32.
Hatano, G., and Inagaki, K. "Two Courses of Expertise." In H. Stevenson, H. Azuma, and K. Hakuta (eds.), *Child Development and Education in Japan.* New York: W. H. Freeman, 1985.
LeVine, R. A., Brazelton, T. B., Dixon, S., Leiderman, P. H., LeVine, S. E., and Richman, A. *Omwana: Infants and Parents in a Gusii Community.* Cambridge, England: Cambridge University Press, forthcoming.
LeVine, R. A., and LeVine, B. *Nyansongo: A Gusii Community in Kenya.* New York: Wiley, 1966.
Moseley, W. H. "Will Primary Health Care Reduce Infant and Child Mortality? A Critique of Some Current Strategies with Special Reference to Africa and Asia." Paper presented at the annual meeting of the International Union for the Scientific Study of Population, Paris, 1983.

Robert A. LeVine is Roy E. Larsen Professor of Education and Human Development at the Harvard Graduate School of Education and professor of anthropology at Harvard University. He has carried out field research in Kenya, Nigeria, and Mexico, and has published extensively on issues in psychological anthropology and human development.

Sarah E. LeVine is research associate in the Laboratory of Human Development at the Harvard Graduate School of Education. She is the author of Mothers and Wives: Gusii Women of East Africa *(1979).*

*While the Yucatec pattern of child care conforms on the whole
to the pattern seen in other agrarian societies, it is currently
becoming destabilized as the society becomes more modern.
Some of the developing customs are maladaptive, at least in
the short run.*

Fertility,
Infant Feeding,
and Change in Yucatán

Gail A. Howrigan

Recent changes in reproductive parameters and infant feeding practices
in rural Yucatán present a challenge to the view of human parental care
as adaptive behavior. During the late 1970s, young women had very large
families with decreasing birth intervals, thus reducing the time and attention given to each infant. Concurrently, they increasingly bottle-fed their
infants, the infants having frequent bouts of gastrointestinal illness due
to poor hygienic conditions. These two related trends continue, despite
explicit parental concern for their infants' health and welfare and despite
a system of child care that in general functions well to meet those concerns. This chapter describes recent trends in reproduction and infant
feeding, documents some of their consequences, and attempts to reconcile
the changes with LeVine's (1974) revised theory of parental behavior.

This study was supported in part by a grant from the U.S. National
Institutes of Mental Health to Beatrice B. Whiting. The author is grateful for
this support, and also wishes to thank Robert A. LeVine for advice and additional
support, T. B. Brazelton, and Suzanne Dixon, the clinic staff at Oxkutzcab, and
the families who participated in this study.

R. A. LeVine, P. M. Miller, and M. M. West (eds.). *Parental Behavior in Diverse Societies.*
New Directions for Child Development, no. 40. San Francisco: Jossey-Bass, Summer 1988.

38

Setting and Sample

The market town of Oxkutzcab in central Yucatán has a population of 12,000, the majority of whom are Yucatec Mayans. Until the 1960s, the milpa system of yearly slash-and-burn corn culture, as old as civilization in Mesoamerica, formed the basis for subsistence. However, government-provided irrigation now makes possible year-round cultivation of fruit for sale. In addition, during the main period of data collection, a large proportion of Mayan men worked in construction jobs away from home and combined wage labor with fruit cultivation. Women help out seasonally with fruit production and vending, but until recently most did not take a major part in agriculture. Married women are expected to devote themselves to child care, household tasks, needlework, hammock-weaving, and the raising of fowl and small animals.

Families live within walled compounds arranged in blocks radiating away from the plaza and market that form the center of town and the residential area for the middle class. As one moves away from the center, one encounters more and more of the small, oval, thatched one-room homes in the Mayan style, and, while the grid pattern is retained, the character subtly changes from urban to rural. On any block, a mixture of residency types is found, though patrilocal-extended and nuclear forms are preferred and are most common. A majority of adults have lived in households of more than one type at different stages of their lives. Young women have their first babies between ages fourteen and twenty-two, and virtually all young couples live in extended households during the early years of family formation.

The findings reported here come from a sixteen-month study in 1978–1979 of young women's preparation for motherhood and of birth order differences in mother-infant interactions in a traditional culture. Data were collected intensively on fourteen mothers of varying parity and their infants, including behavior observations over the first three months and, for a subsample, at six months, as well as nutrition and physical growth data. As part of a census of twenty-nine households, which included those of the study mothers, extensive fertility histories were collected from fifty-four women aged fourteen to seventy-one. In analyzing the fertility data, the women were divided into four age cohorts. The youngest group included twenty-two women aged fourteen to twenty-five; the next youngest, eleven women twenty-six to thirty-five; then nine women thirty-six to forty-five; and, finally, eleven women forty-six and older.

On a three-week return visit in 1983, growth data were obtained for the thirteen surviving study children, who were then about four years old, and interview data were collected about childcare practices and their developmental ethnopsychology for groups of older women and women in midreproductive career. Two stays in the area of five days and three weeks in 1985 and 1986 provided a longer perspective on socioeconomic change and its effects but no formal data collection.

Health and Fertility in Yucatán

In 1978–1979, health facilities included a small, poorly equipped government clinic, staffed by three or four recent medical graduates with little clinical training and an equal number of more experienced nurses. Peasant families brought in their infants for inoculations and came occasionally for their own minor complaints, but they were aware of the staff's inexperience and thus reluctant to make more use of the tiny hospital. For more serious problems, families who could afford it consulted one of the town's four or five private physicians or went to a hospital or private physician in Mérida or in a nearby larger town. A large proportion of medical care was provided by the town's pharmacists, who are quite willing to prescribe from a wide range of modern drugs based on a recital of symptoms (Ferguson, 1981). Finally, there are Mayan health practitioners of several specialized sorts. Certain illnesses, especially of infants, are believed to have supernatural causes, and so can only be treated effectively with Mayan ritual.

During the original study period, environmental sanitation was poor. It is likely to remain so. The poor sanitary conditions, combined with a tropical climate and general ignorance of basic principles of hygiene, provide a very unhealthy setting for bottle-feeding. On the other hand, local physicians can and do provide oral rehydration therapy and antibiotics to treat the gastrointestinal disease that results from such feeding. So, while the environment presents definite hazards to infant health, it also provides the means to save infant lives in most cases.

Current infant mortality rates as reported by the women surveyed were 45.4 deaths and 63.5 deaths per 1,000 live births for the two youngest cohorts of women. While these may be statistically unreliable because of the small sample size, they are in line with the national rate for 1984–1985 of 50 per 1,000 (World Bank, 1987). Infant mortality rates have dropped appreciably during the lifetimes of women who were grandmothers in the 1970s. Ryder (1977) found a rate of 106.6 deaths per 1,000 births for 1936–1970 in a hamlet very near Oxkutzcab, and the 1976 National Fertility Survey (Nagel, 1978) gave a figure of 70 per 1,000 for 1972–1974.

Thus, Yucatec parents in Oxkutzcab face health considerations for their children that are very much a mixture of the modern and the traditional. Their goals for infants—that they should be fat, healthy, and quiet—come from the past. "Modern" feeding methods and Western medicine are broadly accepted. At the same time, the environment still presents considerable hazard, and even the youngest families still resort to traditional Mayan magico-religious healers.

Given how recently infant mortality rates have dropped and how recently it became possible to relinquish total reliance on subsistence agriculture, it is not surprising to find Oxkutzcab's Mayan population still practicing natural fertility. The two younger cohorts of women (those aged fourteen to twenty-five and twenty-six to thirty-five at the time of the survey) reported ages of menarche of 12.9 and 12.3, fairly young by worldwide standards but in line with others reported for different populations in Yucatán (Steggerda, 1941; Tanner, 1978). Average ages of women at the time of first births were 16.7 and 18.9, with a range of fourteen to twenty-two. Birth intervals for the first three or four births averaged 23.2 and 24.7 months, and the mean ages of weaning were 11.0 and 14.1 months. Women aged twenty-six to thirty-five, who have certainly not completed their families, had already experienced 7.0 pregnancies, producing 5.6 live births. These last figures are very close to the completed family sizes found by Steggerda (1941) and Ryder (1976) for earlier periods in Yucatán and by Mata (1978) for a contemporary highland Mayan community in Guatemala.

Education and Class Divisions

With regard to educational attainment and parental perceptions of the value of education and of their children's job prospects, the situation again shows both strong continuity with the past and a growing enthusiasm for newly available choices. Until very recently, parents were (and many still are) content to have their children leave school when they could read, write, do rudimentary sums, and speak Spanish, often at the end of the third or fourth grade. Recently, increasing numbers of boys and girls from Yucatec families attend secondary school (grades seven through nine) and continue beyond that to trade and professional schools.

Since the early postcolonial era, society in Yucatán has been divided into two elements. While the labels have changed over time, the basic ethnic and class divisions have survived. Mestizos, the descendants of the Mayans, are marked by their adherence to traditional dress, the Mayan language, the milpa crop system, and observance of Mayan rituals of field and home. Catrines, the other segment of the population, customarily speak Spanish, dress in European/American garb, and hold "Euro-Mexican" values (Strickon, 1965). With the spread of public schooling and the opening of new occupations (Hansen, n.d.; Thompson, 1974), the division between the groups has become less distinct. More and more Mestizo parents are choosing to rear their children as Catrines.

Patterns of Infant Care

Infant care in rural Yucatán conforms in most ways to the general pattern, described by LeVine in Chapter One, for agrarian societies with high fertility. That is, maternal attention is directed toward keeping the infant healthy and quiet rather than toward reciprocal vocalization and play.

Most of the infant's first year is spent inside the rather dark house, where there is little visual variety, or in the kitchen hut, with poultry, dogs, and older children darting in and out, giving the babies something to watch. In either case, infants spend a large proportion of their time in a hammock, which provides a good vantage point for visual monitoring of surrounding activities and a soothing bed but does not allow the infant to sit or stand independently or to crawl. For the first several days to weeks, infants are kept inside, to protect them, at a time when they are thought particularly vulnerable, from the ill effects of the *aires* (supernatural "winds" the Yucatec believe are everywhere). Visitors from outside the household are kept away from the infant, and the infant only gradually makes the acquaintance of a widening circle of others. The whole family lives in the one-room house, so there is no space especially designated for the baby, nor are there toys, furnishings, or equipment especially intended for the baby, except for an occasional, roughly made infant seat. Later in the first year, caretakers carry the infants around the house lot and into the lanes between blocks, where the babies watch the passing scene and older children at play.

The apparent goal of virtually every care routine is to produce a contented, quiet baby. It is thought to be bad for babies to let them cry, and real crying is rare. The typical pattern of care contributes to the soothing effect. Infants are almost never stressed by overstimulation. Brackbill (1971) and Ambrose (1969) have shown two other characteristics of the care routine of young infants—swaddling and nearly constant rocking—to be highly effective in quieting babies. To induce long naps in older infants so mothers can attend to household chores, mothers carefully and routinely give infants cool baths, powder and dress them in clean clothes, and then feed and rock them to sleep. Between long hours in the hammock and a large proportion of time being held, children's ability to explore the environment and interact with others is considerably constrained.

For the first few months, only mothers and competent caretakers (adult women and girls from the early teens on) attend to the infant. Gradually, younger siblings are employed to help with monitoring, entertaining, and doing simple things for the baby, such as offering a pacifier or rocking. The mother and child caretakers form a team with complementary functions, the child caretakers acting as extensions of the mother's eyes and hands, shuttling between mother and baby with orders to be carried out concerning the baby and information for the mother on the baby's state and needs.

While mothers and other adult females provide very attentive care in terms of frequent feeding, body contact, quick responsiveness to distress, and absence of socialization pressure, such care does not include a great deal of the intense, vocal, affectionate interactional component that seems to be an essential part of "good" care to Western observers. Adult caretakers often visually monitor infants, but their gazes are relatively rarely coordinated with the infants' less frequent looks at the caretakers, as described in Chapter Eight.

This pattern of care fits with the Yucatec conception of the developmental goals of early infancy. When asked what are the most important tasks when dealing with a newborn, mothers of all ages mentioned feeding, cleanliness, vigilance for illness, and prompt attention to any illness symptoms. Beyond these tasks, mothers seem to see their role as that of passive steward of the child's inherent development. They do not feel themselves responsible for the child's characteristics; neither do they seek or feel able to change most infant and child behavior.

The system of child care and developmental beliefs just described has presumably functioned well for centuries. The continuity of these practices in Yucatán is not surprising when we realize that the dramatic drop in the infant mortality rate has taken place in recent memory and that infant deaths, while much less frequent than formerly, are still common enough to make these precautions prudent.

Changes in Fertility and Feeding Practices

While Mexico as a whole seems to be entering a later stage of the demographic transition, with both infant mortality rates and the birthrates dropping, rural Yucatán remains at an earlier stage, where natural fertility is enhanced by several phenomena associated with modernity (Nag, 1980): better medical care and technology, better nutrition, fewer traditional cultural constraints on sexual behavior, greater affluence, the availability of infant feeding alternatives, and the spread of notions of machismo from mainstream Mexican culture.

Fertility histories show that these women's total achieved fertility is increasing, principally because of decreasing infant mortality and shorter birth intervals. As recently as a century ago (Steggerda, 1941), mortality rates were as high as 223 deaths per 1,000 live births and now have decreased to the current rate of approximately 50 deaths per 1,000 births.

The birth intervals in Table 1 were calculated only for the first three or four births to increase comparability across cohorts, and they include all pregnancies, not only those resulting in live births. They show a steady decline from the oldest to the youngest cohort. Furthermore, for the oldest group, the trend across the first four births is for the interval to lengthen, from 26.2 to 33.8 months (Steggerda found a similar

Table 1. Women's Reproductive Parameters

Variables	Age Cohorts			
	14–25	26–35	36–45	46+
n	(21)	(11)	(9)	(11)
Age of menarche	12.9	12.3	12.1	12.4
Age of first birth	16.7	18.9	18.4	18.4
Number of pregnancies	2.3	7.0	8.1	6.5
Birth interval (months)	23.2	24.7	28.0	29.2
Length of lactation (months)	11.0	14.1	19.7	21.9
Infant mortality/ 1,000 live births	45.4	63.5	62.5	33.3

Source: Adapted from Howrigan, 1984, p. 121.

mean and trend forty years ago), whereas the intervals remain about the same or grow shorter for the three younger groups.

Women of all ages were asked what they considered ideal birth-spacing. Most replied that "every two years" was about right, but their answers suggest that they do not have a clear notion of the ideal as distinct from the actual. They do, however, characterize women who bear children especially close together as *añeras*, a term derived from the Spanish *año* (year) and having a clear negative connotation. Mothers who bear children close together are thought to become "used up" *(agotada)* and worn out, while babies are believed to be shortchanged in terms of nutrition and parental attention. Both the new infant and its predecessor are affected, because breast milk is supposedly spoiled by pregnancy and the older child must be weaned.

Contraceptives are easily available to women of all classes in Oxkutzcab, but they are not widely accepted. Fewer than 10 percent of the women surveyed had ever used any mechanical or chemical means of contraception, in contrast with the rate of 31 percent for the Mexican population as a whole (World Bank, 1987) and of 34 percent for women in towns in the population range of Oxkutzcab (Mexican National Fertility Survey, as cited in Nagel, 1978).

If the women in the twenty-six to thirty-five age group, who have already had more children than the oldest group had over their entire reproductive careers, maintain or slightly increase their current birth intervals and experience the same rate of child survival, they will have families numbering eight or more children. These families will be twice the oldest group's family size. How did people feel about this potential for having very large families? When asked about ideal family size, Yucatec women of all ages almost invariably answered, *"Lo que Dios manda"* ("Whatever God wills"). The notion of an ideal number of children, as distinct from the number they actually had, seemed entirely foreign.

Categories of Caretakers. What difference do family size and birth interval make from the child's point of view? Data from the behavior observations provide a partial answer. The kind of caretaker an infant had varied systematically with birth order. Firstborns were cared for almost entirely by their mothers, sometimes with help from older women. Later-borns who came early in their mothers' reproductive careers were very likely to live in extended or joint households, with at least one adult female relative lending a hand in their care. Babies who arrived late in the birth order tended to find themselves in nuclear households, where the only alternate caretakers were older siblings. And each of the three categories of caretakers—mothers, adult women, and children—provided distinctive kinds of care. Mothers' care was characterized by high rates of holding, soothing, rocking, and—relative to the other groups—physical caretaking. Children, on the other hand, did little holding and physical care but had high rates of talking to the babies, of looking at them, and of mutual gazing. Care by adults other than the mother fell somewhere between the other two categories.

The infants with child caretakers came from the largest families and had the busiest mothers. Although the differences failed to reach statistical significance, the total amount of time devoted to feeding the infant was greater in the "mother-only" homes (29 percent) than in the other two categories (19 percent and 17 percent). Mothers were judged to be occupied with work other than care of the subject infant 14 percent of the time in "mother-only" households, 30 percent in "mother-plus-adult" households, and 47 percent in "mother-plus-child" households. As a result, infants of later birth order were much more likely to be left alone in the hammock; the corresponding proportion scores were 3.3, 14.8, and 32.8 percent, respectively. If left alone long enough, the babies became active and then fussy, finally crying if still unattended.

Thus, this constellation of related variables creates a particular pattern of infant care: high parity, which tends to go along with shorter birth intervals; mother with a heavy work load; infant left alone in the hammock a great deal; infant distress; and efforts by caretakers who are likely to be children to distract and calm the infant. The behavior observations did not capture well the qualitative aspects of care; however, much child caretaking seemed episodic, not well related to the infants' needs, and sometimes physically rough. The net differences in the kind of care infants receive would be even greater at later ages; the behavior observations were done at three months, a time when infants are still considered fragile and vulnerable and when the role of child caretakers is still limited.

New Feeding Practices. Infant feeding practices, an issue closely related to birth spacing as well as to infant health and growth, have also undergone recent dramatic change in Yucatán as in many parts of the developing world (Short, 1984). Bottle-feeding has existed in the area at least since World War II, but, while older women resort to it only on an emergency basis, younger women have taken wholeheartedly to bottle-feeding as a supplement to and eventual replacement for breast-feeding. The proportions of women who feed the majority of their babies by exclusively breast have decline from 80 percent for women over forty to 7.7 percent for women aged fifteen to twenty-nine.

The change in feeding method has been accompanied by other changes that have negative implications for infant development. The decrease in the birth interval is paralleled by, and in large part caused by, a significant drop in the age of weaning (from twenty-two to eleven months); the birth of the next child consistently follows seven to twelve months after weaning the older child. The change in age of weaning has gone on despite a general recognition by Yucatec women of the connection between lactation and birth spacing. A number of grandmothers deplored "these young girls who don't care how quickly the babies come—in my day, we nursed and protected ourselves." Younger women were less sure of lactation's efficacy, perhaps because their breast-feeding, now less frequent because combined with bottle-feeding, is in fact less likely to protect them from pregnancy. The longer interbirth intervals of the past were maintained in part by the physiological effects of extended lactation (Short, 1984) as well as by a conscious effort by parents to avoid a new pregnancy that would require weaning an infant too early. In the same way, the present shorter interval is probably due not entirely to earlier weaning but also to the feeling that, with the availability of bottle-feeding, it is no longer necessary to worry about prolonging the supply of breast milk.

Detailed questioning of the fourteen observation mothers about feeding practices after the first few weeks revealed that there is a great deal of variation within the mixed feeding method. Some babies are basically breast-fed on demand but are given a small token portion of powdered formula once or twice a day, as little as eight ounces a day at five months. In these cases, the bottle seems to serve primarily as a symbol of modernity, attesting to the families' interest in doing their best for their offspring. At the other extreme, some babies got as much as thirty ounces a day by bottle but were offered the breast if they awakened at night. This information made it possible to assign a feeding type to each

infant: exclusively breast-fed ("Br"), predominantly breast-fed ("Br +
Bo"), predominantly bottle-fed ("Bo + Br"), exclusively bottle-fed ("Bo").
In Table 2 the infants are arranged by birth interval within feeding types;
the growth measure used is weight as percent of national norm, to make
it possible to integrate boys and girls.

The most striking association is that between feeding type and
illness. The infants noted as having been ill had all had, during the
period of observation (from birth until five to nine months), at least one
bout of diarrhea lasting three or more days and necessitating antibiotic
and rehydration therapy by a physician. *All* of the predominantly bottle-
fed infants and the one exclusively bottle-fed infant had experienced
such illness, and *none* of the predominantly and exclusively breast-fed
ones had (p = 0.005, Fisher's Exact Test, one-tailed). Also, three of the
four infants with low ponderal indices (a ratio of weight to length that
should exceed 2.3) came from the ranks of the bottle-fed infants. Rank
order correlations between feeding type and growth measures at three-
months and four years show that feeding method was very strongly

Table 2. Physical Growth and Health

Subjects	Feeding Method	Birth Interval	Illness	Three-Month Weight % Norm	Three-Month Ponderal Index	Four-Year Weight % Norm
1	Br	58		113.9	3.0	98.2
2	Br	27		112.8	3.07	92.4
3	Br	22		90.5	2.06[a]	76.4
4	Br	—		108.0	2.84	—
5	Br + Bo	29		99.7	3.05	85.5
6	Br + Bo	26		93.8	2.47	81.9
7	Br + Bo	—		102.6	2.46	93.6
8	Br + Bo	—		97.6	2.50	84.4
9	Br + Bo	—		86.3	2.47	86.7
10	Bo + Br	29	x	91.0	2.81	83.7
11	Bo + Br	21	x	93.8	2.65	92.2
12	Bo + Br	14	x	77.9	2.15[a]	71.0
13	Bo + Br	—	x	69.5	2.24[a]	72.8
14	Bo	—	x	78.4	2.31[a]	80.0

[a]A healthy weight-to-length ratio is indicated by a ponderal index that exceeds 2.31.
Source: Adapted from Howrigan, 1984, pp. 167, 169.

related to weight (and length) at three months ($r_s = 0.73$, $p < 0.001$) and still moderately related to weight at four years ($r_s = 0.49$, $p < 0.05$). The growth charts of the study infants reveal that the bottle-fed babies had recurrent bouts of gastrointestinal infections that caused immediate weight losses followed by long periods of slow recovery. The growth curves of the exclusively breast-fed babies, however, in general followed a steady upward course. The relationship between illness and nutritional status sets up a vicious cycle; obviously, the more frequent the bouts of diarrhea, the more poorly children grow. However, recent research in Mexico has also shown prospectively that the greater the degree of preexisting malnourishment, the greater the vulnerability to illness (Sepulveda, Willett, and Munoz, 1988). Thus, mothers' early choices about how to feed their infants can be said to have a lasting influence on the children's growth.

Then why the switch to bottle-feeding, with its negative correlates that seem so obvious to observers? The feeding situation just described has been found in numerous other locations in the developing world, and it presents a challenge to the assumption that any given childcare practice is adaptive in terms of health and survival. The short answer is that bottle-feeding has high social status value in developing areas. The government often encourages its use, as it does in this case by giving powdered formula to the wives of public-sector workers on leaving the clinics where they have given birth. Fathers who work at wage labor jobs in the capital and at coastal resorts are often the agents of change in feeding practices, since they take great pride in being able to provide their children with prestigious and modern food.

Ironically, a second rationale relates to considerations of infant health and survival. LeVine (1974) has pointed out that present parental perceptions are shaped by a culture's past contingencies. The Mayans have for many centuries inhabited an area with very poor soil and uncertain rainfall, with the result that everyone has experienced frequent lean times and occasional seasons of starvation (Ryder, 1977). In this context, parents may seize on bottle-feeding as a way to ensure enough to eat for their infants at all times.

While prestige and survival considerations attract Yucatec parents to bottle-feeding, modern medical facilities weaken the old rationales that dictated breast-feeding. Though infants fall ill more frequently due to bottle-feeding, they are now far less likely to die as a result of gastrointestinal infections because, in a town the size of Oxkutzcab, private doctors and government clinics treat dehydration, the usual proximate cause of infant death, with intravenous fluids. Confidence in modern medical technology seems to have blinded parents to the new risks their feeding choices entail. The changes in infant feeding practices can be seen as an example of the widening acceptance of Euro-Mexican values that social change has brought to Yucatán.

The extent of the generational shift in feelings about infant feeding methods was evident in discussions with groups of women of similar age. Women over forty, most of whom were grandmothers, were firm in their belief that breast milk is more nutritious than anything in a bottle. Beyond nutrition, however, is the idea that in nursing the mother is giving her infant something of herself. The oldest child of one of the observation mothers was a four-year-old girl who was disobedient and unaffectionate with her mother. The grandmother explained that it was because her daughter had not nursed the girl as an infant, "so now she doesn't love her mother." The older women also commented on the connection between bottle use and infant sickliness; younger women did not acknowledge that relationship. They were less articulate about their reasons for using the bottle, but they implied that breast-feeding was old-fashioned and a bit crude, while powdered formula is modern, used by the better-off families, and recommended by doctors—"otherwise, why would they give it out at the clinics?" They did not want their children to be shortchanged of an advantage the upper classes have. Others insisted that bottle-feeding was necessary because they didn't have "enough breast milk." When asked how their grandmothers had managed without powdered formula, they had no answer. While the younger women did not cite maintaining their figures as a reason, as was suggested scornfully by a number of older women, it is true that Catrina dress is considerably more revealing than is the Mestiza *huipil* and that younger women may be absorbing middle-class standards of appearance from the television programs they watch and the *novelas* (soap operas in comic-book form) they read. However, women of all ages seemed to feel that the breast has two functions—to nourish and to comfort, while the bottle offers only nourishment.

The local clinic and private doctors also encourage the use of powdered formula. When they see an undersized infant, whose unsatisfactory growth is in fact often due to illness as a direct result of bottle-feeding, they assume that the mother's breast milk is inadequate and send her off to buy powdered formula at the pharmacy. The formula is very expensive relative to Mestizo families' incomes, so virtually everyone who uses it dilutes the formula with cornstarch.

Conclusion

Why have Yucatecan parents given up an old, adaptive breast-feeding practice in favor of a new, maladaptive bottle-feeding one? It may be that these parents are less sensitive to morbidity than they are to mortality, especially if the means exist to keep the one from leading to the other. Modern medical technology may serve as a safety net, blunting the need for parents to figure out the causal connections between their actions and outcomes. Also, young Yucatec adults consider bottle-feeding desirable because of more exposure to mass media and the models they purvey, having some affluence to acquire what are locally considered luxury goods, and more education and the aspirations that go with it. Mestizo families finally have the means and opportunity to reach for a middle-class life-style, and they seem eager to do so. Yucatec parents may notice that the children of the middle class are bigger, healthier, and more successful in school than their own, and may conclude that middle-class parents must be doing something right. It seems unlikely there will be any improvement in infant feeding practices until the mainstream culture encourages them.

The other major change in the childrearing environment, the increase in family size and corresponding decrease in the birth interval, results in less maternal (and perhaps overall) attention for each infant. Like ill health and poor physical growth, less attention has a developmental effect opposite to the hopes of parents who are adopting a strategy of high investment in each child. Parents seem unlikely to perceive the connection between decreased attention and its negative outcomes, or even to perceive that the attention each child receives has decreased. But the problem may already be waning. The same parental aspirations lead to the realization that education is expensive and that a family can do more with fewer children. While traditional agriculture and folk beliefs about fertility will not disappear soon, many Mayan families already realize that unlimited fertility is incompatible with their present goals.

References

Ambrose, J. A. "Discussion Contribution." In J. A. Ambrose (ed.), *Stimulation in Early Infancy*. New York: Academic Press, 1969.

Brackbill, Y. "Cumulative Effects of Continuous Stimulation on Arousal Level in Infants." *Child Development*, 1971, *42*, 17–26.

Ferguson, A. E. "Commercial Pharmaceutical Medicine and Medicalization: A Case Study from El Salvador." *Culture, Medicine, and Psychiatry*, 1981, *5*, 105–134.

Hansen, A. T. "Changes in the Class System of Mérida, 1825–1935." Unpublished manuscript, University of Yucatán, n.d.

Howrigan, G. A. "Making Mothers from Adolescents: Context and Experience in Maternal Behavior in Yucatán." Unpublished dissertation, Harvard Graduate School of Education, 1984.

LeVine, R. A. "Parental Goals: A Cross-Cultural View." *Teachers College Record*, 1974, *76* (2), 226–239.

Mata, J. L. *The Children of Santa Maria Cauque*. Cambridge: Massachusetts Institute of Technology Press, 1978.

Nag, M. "How Modernization Can Also Increase Fertility." *Current Anthropology*, 1980, *21* (5), 571–587.

Nagel. J. S. "Mexico's Population Policy Turnaround." *Population Bulletin*, 1978, *33* (1) (entire issue).

Ryder, J. W. "Interrelations Between Family Structure and Fertility in Yucatán." *Human Biology*, 1976, *48* (1), 93–100.

Ryder, J. W. "Internal Migration in Yucatán: Interpretation of Historical Demography and Current Patterns." In G. Jones (ed.), *Anthropology and History in Yucatán*. Austin: University of Texas Press, 1977.

Sepulveda, J., Willett, W., and Munoz, A. "Malnutrition and Diarrhea: A Longitudinal Study Among Urban Mexican Children." *American Journal of Epidemiology*, 1988, *127* (2), 365–376.

Short, R. V. "Breast-feeding." *Scientific American*, 1984, *250* (4), 35–41.

Steggerda, M. *Maya Indians of Yucatán*. Carnegie Institute Publication, no. 531. Washington, D.C.: Carnegie Institute, 1941.

Strickon, A. "Hacienda and Plantation in Yucatán: An Historical-Ecological Consideration of the Folk-Urban Continuum in Yucatán." *America Indigena*, 1965, *25* (1), 35–63.

Tanner, J. M. *Fetus into Man: Physical Growth from Conception to Maturity*. Cambridge, Mass.: Harvard University Press, 1978.

Thompson, R. A. *The Winds of Tomorrow*. Chicago: University of Chicago Press, 1974.

World Bank. *World Development Report, 1987*. New York: Oxford University Press, 1987.

Gail A. Howrigan is currently a full-time mother; she is interested in issues of maternal and child health in relation to childrearing practices and has conducted or participated in studies of mother-child interaction and malnutrition in Yucatán.

An examination of Italian parents' goals and childrearing
practices illustrates the role of culture in maintaining practices
that are no longer serving an obvious adaptive function.

Parental Goals and Italian Infant Care

Rebecca Staples New

The data discussed in this chapter were collected during an intensive yearlong field study in central Italy in 1980–1981. The field study focused on the impact of a rapidly changing environment on infant care practices and the mediating effect of larger cultural values during periods of societal transition. This chapter suggests that, environmental pressures notwithstanding, strategies of infant care at any one point in time may reflect not just one but all three of the concerns (for physical well-being, economic viability, and cultural ideologies) itemized in LeVine's (1974) hierarchy and that this is particularly true in societies undergoing major transitions. Likewise, childcare strategies that serve multiple goals have the best chance of surviving when environmental circumstances change.

In the Italian environments observed in this study, parents rely on contemporary versions of customary childcare strategies geared to health maintenance and hazard avoidance, with expressed concerns regarding

This field study was made possible through the cooperation of the Instituto di Psicologia del Consiglio Nazionale di Ricerche, Rome, Italy. Financial support was provided by a Sinclair Kennedy Traveling Grant from Harvard University to the author and by grants to Robert A. LeVine by the Population Council, MacArthur Foundation, and the Spencer Foundation.

R. A. LeVine, P. M. Miller, and M. M. West (eds.). *Parental Behavior in Diverse Societies.*
New Directions for Child Development, no. 40. San Francisco: Jossey-Bass, Summer 1988.

infant health and future economic status. While, in the face of recent demographic changes, such concerns appear unfounded and related strategies no longer necessary, they have been maintained because they conform to a broader Italian ideolgy of infant and child care. Collectively, such caretaking strategies support the Italian cultural mandate to initiate the infant into a social system that regards the family as the major social unit, at the expense of the autonomous individual.

While a peer in many respects of other industrialized Western nations, Italy has managed to retain much of its past, in the form of ancient architecture as well as regional customs and dialects. Despite rapid social changes since the end of World War II, as the country has become more industrialized, the family has managed to retain its position as the major social unit (Keefe, 1977). Italy's unique blending of ancient history, local customs, and contemporary influences provides an excellent opportunity to observe processes of child care in a culture in transition (New, 1984).

The Field Site

"*È brutta, ma c'è lavoro*" ("It's ugly, but there's work"). Thus was Civita Fantera (a pseudonym) described by one of its approximately 16,000 residents. Located an hour north of Rome within the region of Latium, the town is surrounded by a fertile agricultural zone cultivated with fields of tobacco and wheat as well as with vineyards and olive groves. Originally an Etruscan capital city, the town has been identified as possibly the earliest inhabited center of Faliscan territory. Probably chosen as the capital site for its topography, the city was built on a plateau of volcanic sediment created by the eroding banks of the Treia and Maggiore Rivers (Paget, 1973). Although the city was destroyed by the Romans in 241 B.C., it was rebuilt in the ninth century A.D.; and much of the medieval architecture remains in the historic town center, along with an eleventh-century Romanesque cathedral and a papal prison built by San Gallo in the late fifteenth century (Michelin and Company, 1981).

The town remains isolated, geographically as well as socially, from the surrounding countryside. Walls surrounding the plateau have prohibited any natural expansion; thus, in response to moderate but steady population growth (12,957 inhabitants in 1961; 14,339 in 1971; 15,960 in 1981), Civita Fantera has sprawled out beyond two bridges that span the ravines on the north and west sides of town.

The rapid growth of ceramic factories on the town outskirts during the 1970s has served as a major attraction to southern Italian immigrants in search of employment opportunities, and, as a result, entire extended families have relocated within the town. Such factories have been largely responsible for the consistently low unemployment rates (ISTAT, 1983) and for the creation of an industrial economy within an area that remains predominantly agricultural. The sense of economic stability within Civita Fantera is consistent with depictions of other towns in central Italy. Referred to by some as a "third Italy," this socio-geographic region includes those areas of the north and center that are no longer totally reliant on agriculture yet have not become completely industrial; they offer a quality of life that is comfortable and even high at times with respect to the national average (Benigni, Giorgetti, and Sasso, 1987; Donati and Cipolla, 1978).

Health care is available through the local hospital and a community pediatric clinic, as well as through a number of private practices, with a neonatal intensive care unit located twenty-five kilometers (15.5 miles) away. Steadily declining birthrates within the town are on par with the Italian average: eleven births per 1,000 inhabitants in the 1980s compared to twenty per 1,000 in the 1950s (Mitchell, 1976). Infants in this Italian community are statistically no longer considered at risk for survival, as mortality rates, which are also consistent with national figures, have declined dramatically over the past decades; 1982 census figures cite an average of 14 deaths per 1,000 births during the first year of life, as compared with 58 per 1,000 for the period from 1951 to 1955 and 110 per 1,000 during 1941 to 1945 (Somogyi, 1967).

Sources of housing reflect major social distinctions within the community. A majority of working-class families (predominantly southern Italian immigrants) resides in centuries-old apartment buildings that line cobblestoned streets within the historic town center. While most occupancies have been refurbished with amenities such as indoor plumbing and toilet facilities, some have been condemned as unsafe, and many residents remain on the waiting list for new public housing apartments going up on the north side of town beyond the plateau. Middle- and professional-class families, most of whom were born in or around Civita Fantera, typically live in contemporary apartment complexes and suburban homes on the west and north sides of town.

Methods and Procedures

Sample criteria and data collection methods reflect priorities established in the Boston-based study as described in Chapter Six; they include a multimethod approach to the study of infants with older siblings in their home environments.

In addition to ethnographic observations and informal interviews, research procedures included two one-hour naturalistic home observations of all infant behavior and interactions with the infants, parental attitude interviews regarding short- and long-term caretaking goals, and daily routine interviews, during which mothers were asked to recount the previous twenty-four hour period, specifically the household schedule and childcare activities. While this information was sampled at several different age points, only data from the ten-month age point are reported here.

The Sample

The Italian sample consisted of twenty infants and their families, recruited through local birth records as well as the pediatric clinic. The average age of the mothers in this sample was 28.1 (SD = 4.3), the average age of the fathers was 30.9 (SD = 3.9). Mothers had on average of 7.3 years of education (SD = 3.8), while fathers had on average of 8.8 years (SD = 8.8). The average family size of the sample was 2.2 children, and the range was from two to three children.

Sample families were largely representative of town residents in terms of family size, type of housing, employment status, and income. Eleven of the twenty families were of southern Italian ancestry. Housing conditions ranged from two-room apartments within the *Centro Storico* to a sprawling seven-room ranch home in the suburbs, with all but one of the families with southern ancestry residing either in the crowded historic center or in the newer public housing units. Other than type of housing, southern Italian ancestry was not associated with any demographic variables, although there was a tendency for southern Italian families to be characterized by younger mothers (twenty-six as opposed to thirty years old), less educated fathers (seven years of schooling versus ten years), and lower-status father occupations.

The most common source of sample family income was the ceramic industry, where 50 percent of sample fathers were employed. Other occupations reflected the range from working to professional class, including a physician, insurance salesman, radio technician, construction workers, and shop owner.

Average household size (4.6 members) and number of children (2.2) are consistent with the national trend toward smaller nuclear families. There is a significant relationship between family size and income ($p < 0.005$), with all but one of the four families with three children in the middle or professional class.

Community Norms of Social Interaction

The community life within this town was characterized by a high level of social activity, the primacy of the family, and strict adherence to traditional sex roles among adult men and women. An intense sociality permeated all routine daily activities, both in and out of the home. Personal transactions were carried out within full view of surrounding onlookers, and rarely were efforts made to keep exchanges of either a positive or negative nature private. Verbal exchanges with shopkeepers were shared by all customers within earshot, and local pastry shops and liquor bars served as informal gathering places for large groups of adolescents and men.

Family life was nurtured and protected by the community organization of daily routines. Businesses closed down and schoolchildren were dismissed in time to accommodate the midday meal. Even the ceramic factories rotated their early morning and afternoon shifts around this important family time. Extended family networks included maternal and paternal kin, even among the southern Italian immigrants; such kin ties were apparent in daily business, as well as social, activities.

As is the case in other parts of Italy, male and female spheres of activity continue to be clearly articulated; females were assigned to the domestic sphere, and males assumed the role of wage earner, monopolizing the town center and several specific liquor bars (New and Benigni, 1987). Children, on the other hand, intermingled freely with members of both sexes and were regarded as the "tie that binds" adult men and women together. In fact, there was little or no distinction made between activities that were suitable for children versus those exclusive to adults. During outdoor excursions, infants and toddlers were greeted, admired, and encouraged to display such newly acquired skills as throwing a kiss or waving ciao (bye-bye). Numerous encounters between adults and children occurred throughout the course of the day, as children of all ages were integrated into adult social life.

These community norms of social interaction were also reflected in patterns of infant care. While there were some differences between the families of southern Italian background and the others, three overriding features characterized the entire sample's caretaking styles and infant care environments: a wide range of opportunities for infant interactions with individuals other than the mother; a marked uniformity of major parental attitudes and caretaking goals, with a conscious rationale for infant care based on health and assumed physical needs; actual infant care patterns and overall caretaker responsiveness oriented more toward the ongoing family routine and specific goals of parents rather than toward the infant's present state.

The Infant Care Environment

The small nuclear-family configuration belied the actual interpersonal density that characterized infant daily routines. In addition to daily outings with the mother to shop and participate in the customary afternoon stroll, infant care environments themselves were typically populated by a variety of individuals other than mother and infant. Analyses of home observations revealed that infants spent virtually no time alone (5 percent of the observation time) and typically shared their time with at least two other people. Of these people, one was always the mother. While mothers were present in 100 percent of the observations, infants spent only about a third of their time (31 percent) with just their mothers. The rest of the time (64 percent) they were with their mothers and at least one other person. In fact, for almost half of that time, two or more other people were present during the observation.

This high level of social density was apparent throughout the first year of life, and it is worth noting that a vast majority of these visitors were not strangers to the infant but were intimately acquainted with the lives of family members. In spite of the predominantly nuclear-family household arrangements (only three widowed grandparents resided within the sample family households), most of the visitors observed (74 percent) were extended family members, all of whom lived within the same community. Friends and neighbors were also common to the infant care scene, reflecting the public quality that was typical of community social norms.

High social density does not always translate into attention for an infant. For example, Chisholm's (1981) study of the Navaho revealed a low amount of infant-directed behavior amid high social density. Yet infants in this Italian sample received a considerable amount of attention in and out of the home, from a number of socializing agents other than the mother. Figure 1 shows that others were engaged in social interaction with the baby 74 percent of the time (forty-four minutes of the hourlong observation) on the average, while the baby was engaged in social interaction with others 70 percent of the time (forty minutes of the hourlong observation) on the average. Of this social time, 55 percent (thirty-two minutes) was joint social interaction time.

Many of the infant-directed activities by those outside the nuclear family involved physical and verbal stimulation, and such interactions often included more than one partner for the infant. Such encounters commonly included practicing of newly developing physical and social skills, with much praise and recognition for the well-dressed and well-behaved child (*"Che bello, che buono"*). These verbal praises were delivered in a high-pitched stylistic fashion that was particularly common among older women.

Children of all ages and both sexes were attentive to infants and frequently attempted to help those who were learning to walk. Although often discouraged by their mothers, siblings assumed the responsibility of teaching their younger brother or sister to say *"no-no"* as they helped them playfully slap others in the group. Adults and children engaged infants in games of peek-a-boo and patti-cake and were observed teach-

Figure 1. Social Interactions Between Infants and Others as Proportions of the Observation Period

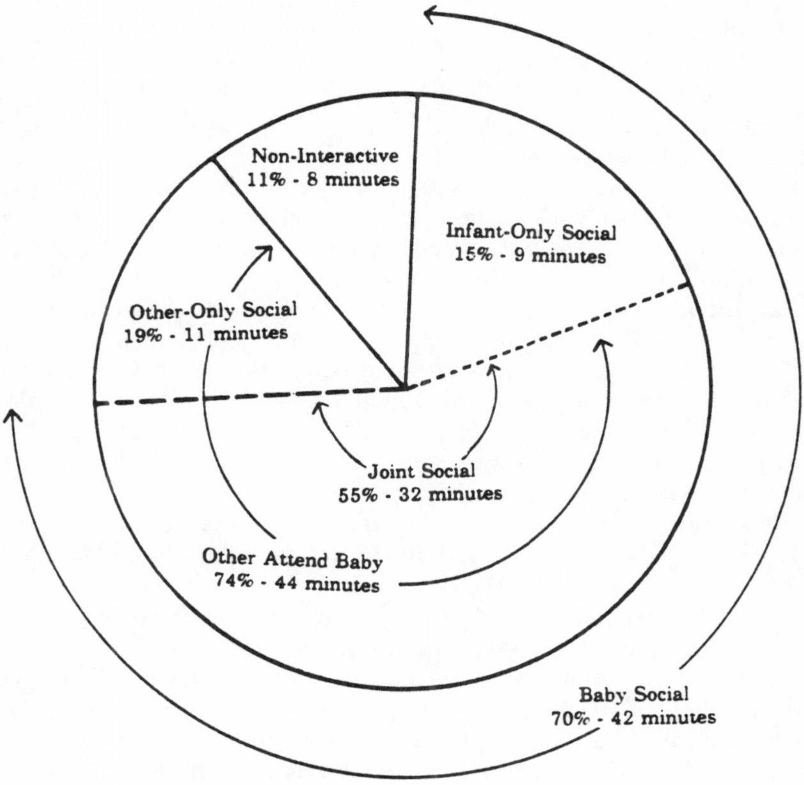

Non-Interactive
11% - 8 minutes

Infant-Only Social
15% - 9 minutes

Other-Only Social
19% - 11 minutes

Joint Social
55% - 32 minutes

Other Attend Baby
74% - 44 minutes

Baby Social
70% - 42 minutes

Source: New, 1984.

ing infants as young as four months to open and close the fist in the traditional gesture of greeting, ciao. Siblings and their friends were most likely of all interaction partners to share toys and other objects with infants.

Equally apparent features of many infant interactions with adults included vigorous handling as well as teasing, both of which often resulted in more tears than laughter on the part of the infant. Games of this type involved adults playfully but forcefully spanking infants or removing an object (such as a pacifier) from the infant's grasp and holding it just out of reach. With older infants, adults would offer candy, only to feign mock surprise and say that there was none; or point to the door, declaring, *"Ecco viene Papa!"* ("Here comes Daddy!"), only to laugh and declare, *"Non c'e piu!"* ("He isn't here anymore!") when the infant had crawled or toddled over to peek through the vacant doorway. In each of the above cases, the concluding scenario would likely entail a swooping of the tearful infant with laughter from the onlookers, followed by hugs and kisses.

As a result of this frequent teasing and social activity, sample infants appeared to develop a remarkable tolerance for high levels of stimulation. Even infant sleep periods often occurred in noisy social settings. Daytime naps were likely to be in someone's lap or in a carriage in the middle of the kitchen, lasting until such time as someone decided to wake the infant with a jiggle or a pinch on the cheek. At night, infants commonly slept in the same room as their parents regardless of the availability of separate sleeping spaces. It was considered unkind to put an infant to sleep alone in a room, just as it was unfair to separate the infant from the rest of the household during social events.

In spite of the large amount of attention directed toward the sample infants, play sessions as defined in U.S. studies (in which the child is in charge of the situation) were relatively infrequent, accounting on the average for less than four minutes per hour of observation. For the most part, play was initiated and terminated at the discretion of the adult. While all sample infants appeared to have some toys of their own, they were used most often as distractions during caretaking tasks. At a time when the child's interest in the properties of the physical world could be expected to be rapidly expanding, object-mediated activities represented less than 4 percent of all behaviors directed to sample infants. Opportunities for infant locomotor activity were also infrequent. Infants were typically observed in someone's lap or in some form of apparatus (walker, playpen, high chair), with unrestricted floor time limited to approximately one fourth (26 percent) of the total observation period.

General characteristics of infant social interactions, in sum, featured a high level of social density, including a great deal of physical and verbal attention to the infant, with adults and other children frequently determining the type and extent of involvement. Purposeful teasing of the infant was commonplace, as was the waking of a sleeping infant if someone wanted to play. Independent exploration of the environment or manipulation of objects was rarely encouraged and frequently inhibited. While southern Italian families were more likely to have greater numbers of children present in the infant care environment and were less likely to place infants on the floor, these characteristics were significant features of a vast majority of the infant care environments.

Patterns of Mother-Infant Interaction

Maternal patterns of interaction with infants were similar to others' in that mothers remained in charge of the exchange; such interactions were distinct, however, in their focus. Mother-infant interactions were typically centered on one of three tasks: feeding, grooming, or dressing the infant.

Mothers performed virtually all of the feeding and physical childcare tasks (85 percent of feeding; 84 percent of bathing, grooming, and dressing), and they were the least likely of all interaction partners to engage infants with objects. Since mothers remained the primary interaction partner, even given the frequent presence of other socialization partners, infants were more likely to be observed in one of those physical caretaking settings (representing 17 percent of the total observation period) than either play or object-mediated activity. This pattern of behavior was consistent with mothers' interpretations of the maternal role. When asked to describe the nature of their role during infancy, mothers consistently mentioned physical care needs: proper feeding, hygiene, and carefully controlled exposure to fresh air. These short-term goals were translated into observable caretaking strategies, and each mother carried out these physical care tasks with confidence and efficiency, often in spite of infant preferences to the contrary.

Infant feedings were aligned with family meals at approximately four-hour intervals, and there were few accommodations made for the infant who was hungry ahead of schedule or even for the infant who was sleeping when it was time to eat. A fat baby was considered a healthy baby, and most mothers preferred to spoon-feed their infants well into the second year rather than risk an inadequate meal as the result of self-feeding efforts. The cultural value attached to *la bella figura* extended downward to infancy, and the physical appearance of male and female infants assumed a priority that often reinforced the limitations of locomotor activity. Elaborate efforts at grooming and dressing infants preceded most outdoor excursions, and siblings and neighbor children were regularly warned not to get the infant dirty. Toddlers were not allowed out of their carriages when their mothers stopped for conversation in the park, which also bore no evidence of childproofing. The priority on carefully groomed infants far exceeded any concern for the provision of independent exploration of the physical environment, indoors or out.

In addition to their primary role as the infant's physical caregiver, mothers also served as a major source of infant stimulation. The most frequently observed maternal behavior other than visual monitoring of her infant was talking, occurring in 39 percent of her infant interactions. Mothers were also quick to acknowledge although not necessarily to comply with infant signals. Infant frets and cries were consistently followed (at a rate of 77 percent within the following five-second period) by looks, talking, and holding, with southern Italian mothers somewhat less likely to talk following infant crying; infant nondistress vocalizations were almost as rapidly acknowledged (67 percent within the subsequent five-second interval). A not-infrequent mother-infant exchange would include infant gestures or requests for something, with the mother responding verbally without acquiescing to the infant's demands.

While there was clear acknowledgment and encouragement of the infant as a member of the family social order, there was little recognition of the infant's increasing capabilities for autonomous behavior. In spite of mothers' expressed rationale for infant care based on health and assumed physical needs, actual infant needs were often disregarded in favor of family routines. The unilateral relationship of the child to the family was thus maintained.

Ũno Fa Quello Che Puo (One Does What One Can)

How do these infant-care strategies relate to sample parents' long-term goals for their children? Mothers' and fathers' long-term goals fell into one of the following three categories: Financial security, typically in the form of a "good job," was mentioned by either the mother or the father in fifteen out of twenty families. A good education was mentioned by one or both parents in fourteen out of twenty families as either a primary goal or the key to ensure that their children's lives would be "better than mine." Both of these goals seem to relate to the second goal in LeVine's (1974) model: that of ensuring the economic viability of one's children. Other goals were related to good health, to the family (including a good marriage, respect for parents, and cooperative relationships among siblings) and morality, specifically honesty. These goals seem to relate more to LeVine's third goal.

Evidence of the economic concerns should not be readily apparent in infant care practices, according to LeVine's original model, given that training for economic participation most often takes place following infancy. Yet a number of infant care practices, including the restriction of infant mobility and overall concern with infant cleanliness and feeding, combined with pressures on conformity in older children, are reminiscent of other studies of working-class families where economic security and educational opportunities are lacking (Kohn, 1969; Lozoff and Brittenham, 1979; Moss and Jones, 1977).

The expressed concern for the health and physical well-being of their children was congruent with mothers' short-term goals and somewhat consistent with actual childcare practices during infancy. While sample infants were generally healthy and medical care was available within the town, mothers frequently talked about health-related issues and adhered to local remedies for ensuring infant health (such as having the infant wear a hat to ward off the March sun). It is worth noting that sample grandparents, who represent key figures in the daily routines of infants, were raising their families during the 1940s and 1950s, at a time when infant mortality rates (United Nations Statistics Office, 1957) were easily double that of other industrialized nations (for example, seventy-two per 1,000 births during 1948 as compared with thirty-two per 1,000 for the U.S.). Perhaps even more to the point, over half of the sample families interviewed mentioned a death during infancy of either a parent's or grandparent's sibling. The sheer presence of elderly extended family members in the infant care environment serves to maintain some version of infant care practices that previously served them well, such as protection from hazards and careful monitoring of food to ensure sufficiency. These individuals have even aided in the transition to more contemporary forms of infant care when such changes appeared consistent with their goals. Grandmothers, for example, reportedly played a major role in many mothers' decision to switch from breast- to bottle-feeding so that the milk intake could be carefully monitored (Benigni, conversation with the author, January 1981). In short, it seems likely that many if not most of the individuals involved in infant care in this sample were operating with a heightened sense regarding infant vulnerability.

To that end, many features of the Italian infant care setting are somewhat reminiscent of settings with high infant mortality rates. Constant physical contact between infant and caregiver has been updated in the form of restricting infant mobility through contemporary restraining apparatuses. Maternal behavior includes high responsiveness rates to crying. While feeding is no longer a frequent response to infant distress, it is clearly of major concern to mothers, particularly in the sense that mothers work hard to ensure that infants ingest what the mothers define as "enough" food. Finally, while there is ample treatment of the infant as a socially responsive individual, there is little effort made at developing truly reciprocal patterns of communication between infant and caregiver.

Yet these patterns of infant care are not without emphasis on other culturally distinctive beliefs and values, specifically those associated with the growing child's social and emotional relationships within the family, including the extended family network. An even greater mandate than that of environmental concerns seems to govern strategies of infant care in this Italian community—a mandate that has held constant in spite of (or perhaps because of) fluctuating socioeconomic conditions throughout Italy: the development and maintenance of the individual's ties to the family.

This emphasis on family solidarity has been extensively documented throughout Italy (Moss, 1981; Peristany, 1977). It should also be noted that this conception of *la famiglia* goes beyond those nuclear-family members sharing a household. In spite of a clear demographic trend away from the extended family (Mabilia, 1980), current research suggests that ties with kin outside the nuclear family continue to be a major feature of family life throughout much of Italy (Paci, 1982;

62

Saraceno, 1981; Siebert, 1984). In this sample, the constant reminders of the developing infant's immature status with respect to the family hierarchy may be seen as simultaneously encouraging a reliance on other family members to see to his or her welfare and discouraging autonomous behavior or independent daily routines. This pairing of values, which seems to pervade the overall infant care system of the twenty sample families, may be seen as appropriate enculturation in a society that has relied for centuries on the strength and ubiquity of the family.

References

Benigni, L., Giorgetti, A., and Sasso, S. "The Ecology of Fathering in a Small Italian Town." In J. Valsiner (ed.), *Cultural Context and Child Development.* New York: Ablex, 1987.
Chisholm, J. "Residence Patterns and the Environment of Mother-Infant Interaction Among the Navaho." In T. Field, A. Sostek, P. Vietze, and P. H. Leiderman (eds.), *Culture and Early Interaction.* Hillsdale, N.J.: Erlbaum, 1981.
Donati, P., and Cipolla, C. *La Donna Nella Terza Italia.* Rome: Editrice A.V.E., 1978.
Instituto Nazionale di Statistica (ISTAT). "Population and Movement of Population in the Commune from 1964 to 1980." *Yearbook of Demographic Statistics, 1982 and 1983.* Rome, Italy: Instituto Nazionale di Statistica, 1983.
Keefe, E. K. *Area Handbook for Italy.* Washington, D.C.: American University Foreign Area Studies, 1977.
Kohn, M. L. *Class and Conformity: A Study in Values.* Homewood, Ill.: Dorsey Press, 1969.
LeVine, R. A. "Parental Goals: A Cross-Cultural View." *Teachers College Record,* 1974, *76* (2), 226–239.
Lozoff, B., and Brittenham, G. "Infant Care: Cache or Carry?" *Journal of Behavioral Pediatrics,* 1979, *95* (3), 478–483.
Mabilia, M. "Family Structure and the Use of Nicknames in a Community of Upper Padua." *Rassegna Italiana di Sociologia,* 1980, *21* (4), 585–605.
Michelin and Company (eds.). *Tourist Guide: Italy.* London: Michelin Tyre Company, 1981.
Mitchell, B. R. *European History Statistics: 1750–1970.* New York: Columbia University Press, 1976.
Moss, H. A., and Jones, S. "Relations Between Maternal Attitudes and Maternal Behavior as a Function of Social Class." In P. H. Leiderman, S. R. Tulkin, and A. Rosenfeld (eds.), *Culture and Infancy: Variations in the Human Experience.* New York: Academic Press, 1977.
Moss, L. W. "The South Italian Family Revisited." *Central Issues in Anthropology,* 1981, *3* (1), 1–16.
New, R. "Italian Mothers and Infants: Patterns of Care and Social Development." Unpublished doctoral dissertation, Harvard Graduate School of Education, 1984.
New, R., and Benigni, L. "Italian Fathers and Infants: Cultural Constraints on Paternal Behavior." In M. E. Lamb (ed.), *The Father's Role: Cross-Cultural Perspectives.* Hillsdale, N.J.: Erlbaum, 1987.
Paci, M. *La Struttura Sociale Italiana.* Bologna, Italy: Il Mulino, 1982.
Paget, R. F. *Central Italy: An Archeological Guide.* Parkridge, N.J.: Noyse Press, 1973.

Peristany, J. G. (ed.). *Mediterranean Family Structures.* Cambridge, England: Cambridge University Press, 1977.

Saraceno, C. "Family Models." In *Ritrato di Famiglia degli Anni '80.* Bari, Italy: Laterza, 1981.

Siebert, R. *Le Ali di un Elefante.* Milan, Italy: Franco Angeli, 1984.

Somogyi, S. *La Mortalita nei Primi Cinque Anni di Eta in Italia (1863–1962).* Palermo, Italy: Ingrano, 1967.

United Nations Statistics Office. *Demographic Yearbook.* New York: United Nations, Department of Economics and Social Affairs, 1957.

Rebecca Staples New is assistant professor of child and family studies at the College for Human Development, Syracuse University.

*The childcare practices of mothers in suburban Boston
seem to reflect the mothers' emphasis on cultural values
such as independence and exploration to further cognitive
development.*

The Socialization of Infants in Suburban Boston

*Amy L. Richman, Patrice M. Miller,
Margaret Johnson Solomon*

Psychologists are increasingly aware that infant development takes place within a social context. Studies of fathers' involvement in childrearing (Lamb, 1987) and sibling relationships (Dunn, 1983; Dunn and Kendrick, 1982) represent efforts to look at the larger family system in order to understand the developing child. However broadly the social context is defined, rarely are the influences of our own cultural beliefs and values on the parent-child relationship considered. In this chapter we will examine the role of parental values in determining childrearing practices among middle-class families in the Boston area.

Many aspects of parent-child relationships are in fact affected by cultural values. For example, Super and Harkness (1981) suggest that the notion of "difficult" temperament represents an interaction between certain characteristics of the infant and characteristics of the cultural context in which the infant develops. Just as we can think of a potential mis-

This study was supported by a grant from the Spencer Foundation to Robert A. LeVine, Harvard Graduate School of Education. The authors are particularly grateful to the families whose yearlong participation in the study made this chapter possible.

R. A. LeVine, P. M. Miller, and M. M. West (eds.). *Parental Behavior in Diverse Societies.*
New Directions for Child Development, no. 40. San Francisco: Jossey-Bass, Summer 1988.

match between a certain mother and baby, there can be a mismatch between a particular constellation of infant characteristics and the culturally defined characteristics of the caretaking environment. For example, in a culture where infants are tied to the mother's body with a cloth and carried out to the fields or to the market, an infant who resists or actively protests being carried may be viewed as difficult. In another cultural setting where infants are left at home in the care of a grandmother or other adult female or where infants go to group daycare centers, an infant who resists being carried does not represent such a mismatch with the caretaking environment. In settings with multiple caretakers, sociability with these caretakers may be an important component of an optimal match between the infant and the caretaking environment. An appreciation of the influences of culture on childrearing values and parenting behavior will help us to understand the deeper meanings that these behaviors have for the parents and children that we study.

Often studies of cultural beliefs and childcare practices are conducted in societies so exotic or so different from our own that it is not at all surprising to discover different values and behaviors. Sometimes it is difficult to get any insight into our own beliefs and practices from these studies. For this reason, several of us have applied the comparative method to studies in the United States and western Europe, countries similar to each other on many dimensions of modernization. In this chapter we will illustrate, for a sample of U.S. middle-class families, how the structuring of the childcare environment is related to culturally defined parental goals and attitudes toward development.

Living Amid Rapid Social Change

The effect of culture on the maternal role and parenting values surfaces when we look at the women who constitute the U.S. sample and how we located them. We designed the Boston study to obtain observational data on mother-infant interaction that could be compared with several other cultures yet still be representative of Boston middle-class families. This raised issues about several demographic variables. For example, we noted that most children in the world were not firstborn; indeed, at that point in time, most children in the U.S. were not firstborn. However, much research in social development, and therefore much of the theorizing in social development, is founded on the results of laboratory studies and home studies of firstborn infants. Because a comparative study would be most useful if the effect of first-time parenting could be eliminated, we selected a sample of later-born infants whose mothers were their primary caretakers.

We contacted several pediatricians and obstetricians in the western suburbs of Boston and obtained permission to phone patients with infants. On initial phone calls to potential subjects, we learned that middle-class women were realizing their parental roles in various ways. As we anticipated, a portion of mothers were employed and were returning to work when their infants were three to six months of age. However, in 1979, when we began this study, the decision to have a second or third child sometimes brought with it a family decision that the mother was going to be the primary caregiver during the first year of life or longer. It was these families who were included in our study.

During interviews, we discovered that these middle-class families were surrounded by rapid social change similar in some ways to what LeVine and LeVine, in Chapter Three, describe for the Gusii sample and Howrigan in Chapter Four, describes for the Yucatec Mayan community. Mothers of infants who were not employed outside the home lived next door to mothers who had returned to work. In neighborhoods where economic and educational indicators were similar, individual families were beginning to work out individual solutions to accomplishing their childrearing goals as well as their often competing goals for economic security.

The twenty mothers in this study were twenty-seven to thirty-eight years old, with a mean age of thirty-one. They were, on the average, twenty-five at the birth of their first child, and the mean birth spacing between children was four years. The second- or later-born children who were the subjects of the study were either four months old ($n = 9$) or ten months old ($n = 11$) at the beginning of the study.

Three sources of data are reported on here. Each infant was observed at three different age points, for a total of four hours at each age point. Since each group of infants was observed at ten months, the data from the ten-month age point are reported here. During these observations, mothers were asked to follow their normal routines. The observer recorded the behaviors seen during infants' interactions with whoever was present, as well as basic setting information, such as the context of the interaction (play, feeding, diaper change, infant alone), whether the infant was being held or not, and whether the infant was in some kind of apparatus (playpen, infant seat, high chair, or walker). Each mother also participated in extensive interviews, including an interview about their short-term and long-term goals as a parent and a daily routine interview in which they were asked to recount the events of the previous twenty-four hours (particularly the events relating to care of the subject child).

In this sample, mothers were able to articulate some of their goals; however, we have found through cross-cultural research that it is often difficult for mothers to articulate those aspects of development that they value most highly. To circumvent this problem, LeVine (1981) developed a technique of interviewing mothers about behavior problems that exist in their culture and ones that have been identified elsewhere. The interview includes questions about the causes of such behaviors, about whether or not a parent should try to change the child's behavior, and about methods for doing so. A version of this interview was used for this study. We also added a section about long-term goals for development. It is important to note that the questions in this interview were open-ended. The mothers were asked questions about their goals and given the opportunity to state in their own words what those goals were.

Parental Goals

Long-Term Parental Goals. When questioned about values and goals for their children, mothers in our study expressed three goals consistently. Nineteen out of twenty mothers mentioned the importance of independence: Children should make their own decisions and establish separate existences. Mothers stated that it is the parent's task to help their children achieve that end. Seventeen out of twenty mentioned the importance of certain inner psychological qualities: Children should be happy regardless of the material conditions of their lives. The third goal involved relationships with others: Children should be generous, honest, and respectful of the rights of others; seventeen of the mothers mentioned this concern.

We place these three goals under LeVine's (1974) third category of parental goals: the development of the child's behavioral capacity for maximizing cultural values other than those related to economic self-maintenance. According to LeVine's hypotheses, parents focus on concerns for secondary goals such as the child's emotional security in situations where economic survival seems assured. The Boston case suggests a different relationship between these two goals: that parents in the United States stress general cultural values because they feel that they have so little control over the specific economic path their children will follow. While all of the Boston mothers assumed that their children would be able to gain some kind of economic self-maintenance, they expressed complete uncertainty about the particular form that this self-maintenance would take. Unlike the Gusii mother who sees obedience training as closely tied to her child's economic success, the U.S. mother has no formulaic strategy for her child's economic security. Mothers instead felt that they might be both unable and unwilling to have much of an effect on their children's career choices. This attitude is related both to the unpredictability of the future and to their acknowledgment of their children's rights and needs to make independent choices. In the face of this uncertainty, mothers expressed the importance of their children acquiring other values that would contribute to their success—or at least to their happiness if their economic success were in question.

Goals for the Infancy Period and Their Impact on Childrearing Practices. Mothers were asked about several short-term goals for the day-to-day management of infant care. We have chosen to discuss three goals that have been identified in previous work by LeVine (1974, 1977) and Caudill and Plath (1966) on the relationship between cultural values and childcare practices. These short-term goals are: protection against hazards, the management of eating, and the management of sleeping. We will show how the structure of the childcare environment is related both to the mothers' stated long-term parental goals and to these short-term goals for infancy.

LeVine (1974) posits that the practice of carrying infants and toddlers during most of their waking hours functions as an accident preventive in settings where there are potential hazards such as cooking fires and streams. LeVine originally formulated this hypothesis with the African setting in mind. To what extent can the hazard avoidance hypothesis be shown to describe U.S. childrearing as well? The middle-class home in the United States is not by any means hazard free. Many of our modern conveniences, such as stoves, electrical outlets, stairs, medicines, household chemicals, electrical appliances, and running water, constitute serious health hazards for young children. Indeed, household accidents are among the leading causes of death for U.S. children aged zero to two years. In the first year of life, 66 percent of deaths for boys and 30 percent of deaths for girls are due to accidents. In the second year, the accident mortality figures are 56 percent and 38 percent, respectively ("Accident Mortality . . .," 1975). Most childhood accidents occur in or near the home, and, while nearly a quarter of them are motor-vehicle-related, the majority of childhood accidents are related to the household hazards mentioned above (Gallagher and others, 1982).

The Boston mothers' strategies for dealing with these hazards are quite different from those used by the Gusii and reflect the tension between the two goals of infant survival and the development of independence. The U.S. mothers' first strategy is childproofing, or rearranging the environment so that potential hazards are removed. A second strategy is to restrict the child's movement. This is done quite differently from the Gusii, who restrain the child primarily through holding. In the United States, mothers either hold the infant; place the child in a high chair, infant seat, or playpen; or restrict the child's movement to certain parts of the home within which she or he is allowed freedom of movement. A third method of accident prevention is to teach the infant, even in the first year of life, what the hazards are, thus assigning some responsibility to the child for its own safety. While both childproofing and teaching the child about hazards were observed in our sample families, we will focus here on efforts to restrict the child's movement.

The degree to which infants are held by their mothers, siblings, or others in the Gusii and U.S. samples varies greatly. Whereas Gusii infants were held during approximately 80 percent of the observations at age three to six months and, on the average, in half of the observations at age nine to twelve months, infants in the U.S. sample were held only 45 percent of the time in the earliest observations and less than 20 percent of the time by the end of the first year.

Infants in the United States in the first year of life also spend a considerable amount of time in various sorts of "containers," such as high chairs and playpens—on the average, 39 percent of the time at age four months and 29 percent at age ten months. These pieces of modern equipment seem to fulfill some of the same functions as holding in that they keep the infant safe from potential household hazards, and they prop the infant in an upright position so that he or she has the opportunity to observe what's going on in the environment. Note also that U.S. infants have their activities restricted by either holding or containerization about the same amount of time that Gusii infants are held (84 percent of the time for infants during the earliest observations and 49 percent by the end of the first year). Yet the practice of putting children in containers is quite distinct from being carried, for it precludes physical contact with others. It may also allow an infant to be left safely alone for extended periods of time.

One curious point about the use of these containers is that they are not used to restrict the infant's movements at all times. At an age when the infant is capable of moving around and thereby encountering dangers (around ten months), mothers increasingly took the children out of these containers and encouraged them to explore. Furthermore, most families owned baby equipment, such as walkers, especially designed to help the prelocomotor child master the environment. These walkers were used even though pediatricians and early childhood specialists have warned parents about the potential safety hazards they pose. Mothers justified the use of walkers and free floor time by stressing the importance of exploration, especially to the child's cognitive and emotional development. While mothers were aware of the potential for accidents in allowing the infant to explore the environment, they did not seem anxious once certain precautions were taken. Allowing the infant freedom of movement within a small, safe environment (that is, a childproofed area) was the preferred means for integrating two competing goals: that of hazard prevention with that of intellectual development.

Whiting (1981), in his study of infant carrying practices, has demonstrated that these practices are considerably constrained by the physical environment—most notably, by the lowest temperature during the coldest month. But, even when physical environments are similar, we still see cultural variations in infant care practices based on parental values. For example, different values are evident in the way Italian versus U.S. parents regulate infant sleeping and eating.

In contrast to the Italian practices described in Chapter Five, most U.S. infants, after the neonatal period, slept in their own beds and, in most cases, in their own rooms. In those families where the infants shared a room, it was always with an older sibling rather than with the parents. Infants between four and ten months old woke around seven in the morning; they napped twice during the day and went to bed around eight in the evening. In every case, infants were removed from the social stimulation of the dinner table or family room activity to their own quiet bedrooms at an identifiable bedtime, between seven and eight o'clock, and participated in elaborate bedtime routines that could include rocking, feeding, or reading a story. A few of the infants were put to bed before the family's evening meal and did not, for example, get to see their fathers as a result. Mothers were very concerned that their infants get enough sleep (on average, fourteen hours per day) and persevered in their efforts to get their infants to nap or to go to bed, even in cases where the infants showed great resistance such as prolonged crying. The struggles about sleep did not end at bedtime. About half the infants woke at one or two in the morning on a regular basis, a situation that most mothers identified as quite undesirable. Mothers gave many reasons for insisting on keeping to a sleep schedule, such as the baby doesn't know when she's tired, or children will develop bad sleeping habits if they are not put on a schedule during infancy. Many mothers also justified the importance of getting infants to go to bed in terms of its effect on their own lives and the benefit for the family, such as mothers need their sleep, or parents need time for themselves, and so on.

Super and Harkness (1981) compare infant sleep and wake patterns in a rural East African community and a metropolitan Boston community. Their findings for the Boston sample are similar to those reported here. Super and Harkness suggest that parental insistence on so much sleep, especially through the night, may be taxing the infant to the limits of its physiological adaptability. They interpret the temporal organization of infant sleep and wakefulness as shaped to coincide more with the temporal organization of parents' lives than with the characteristics or needs of infants.

Maternal attitudes toward eating problems were quite different. Mothers in general felt that infants can and should regulate their own eating habits. While all recognized the importance of a proper diet for the health and survival of the child, they felt that trying to change a child's eating habits might only create problems. At both four and ten months of age, infants were fed about six times a day, which was, according to their mothers, when they were hungry and not necessarily at a scheduled time. Because infants ate "when they were hungry," they quite often ate separately from the rest of the family.

We can see that infant eating is managed differently from sleeping in these Boston families. Mothers say that they can and should control infants' waking and sleeping schedules even over the infant's strong protests, but they will not force infants to eat. In both areas the theme of independence is expressed, albeit in different ways. Infants are allowed to regulate their own eating schedules and the amounts ingested. While infants are forced to conform to parentally imposed sleep schedules, the practice of sleeping in their own beds and, usually, in their own rooms reflects a degree of physical separation from other family members. The consequence of both their eating and sleeping schedules is that many of the U.S. infants' activities are separate from those of other family members, and their opportunities for participating in social interaction are reduced.

Children must learn very early in our society that there is a sharp demarcation between social time and time alone. Time alone includes bedtime, sleeping in one's own bed, learning to go to sleep by yourself, and so on. In contrast, during social times, U.S. children enjoy a great deal of attention from parents. There is a high intensity to the interactions between parents and infants that one does not find in most other cultural contexts (Dixon, Tronick, Keefer, and Brazelton, 1981). Thus, a young child develops high expectations for attention during social interaction but also must learn to delay her or his needs for such interaction until the time is right. The tremendous pressure that we place on our children to separate and to develop autonomy may produce emotional side effects. It may in young children produce fears of separation and nightmares or, on the other hand, excessive feelings of distance from others. Still, these childcare practices are consistent with culture-specific long-term goals—namely, training for independence, "happiness," and good relationships with others.

As Rebecca New describes in Chapter Five, Italian mothers' attitudes and behaviors concerning the management of infant sleeping and eating are almost the reverse of the American pattern. These two aspects of infant care allow social interaction with family members for the Italian infant but limit opportunities for social interaction for the U.S. infant. They allow initiative for the infant in the United States but limit it for the infant in Italy.

In the daily routines of the Boston families, we observed many common rituals concerning food, bedtime, play, and social interaction. Mothers reflected on certain of these childcare practices as purposeful and of long-term consequence. By the time infants were four months of age, mothers had established patterns of interaction and childcare routines that were comfortable and predictable. They were experiencing positive feedback from their infants in terms of their parental goals as their infants became more sociable, more autonomous, and more active. Social interactions between mothers and infants themselves communicated to mothers that they were doing "a good job." In other words, the familiar childcare routines were self-reinforcing.

The findings from the Boston study are important when we acknowlege how many mothers are currently balancing multiple roles and seeking to realize sometimes competing parental and economic goals. As the U.S. Department of Labor (1988) statistics show, mothers of young infants are now the fastest-growing segment of the labor force. Currently 50 percent of mothers of children under one year of age are returning to work. Mothers working outside the home may share the culturally defined parental goals expressed by the mothers in the Boston study; however, they must often redefine or establish new childcare routines and practices because the traditional practices no longer work. We have moved rapidly from a system of childcare where mothers derived rather immediate feedback concerning their goals to a set of childcare practices where it will be very difficult for mothers to evaluate if they are "doing a good job."

References

"Accident Mortality at the Preschool Ages." *Statistical Bulletin*, 1975, *56* (5), 7–9.
Caudill, W., and Plath, D. "Who Sleeps by Whom? Parent-Child Involvement in Urban Japanese Families." *Psychiatry*, 1966, *32*, 12–43.
Dixon, S., Tronick, E., Keefer, C., and Brazelton, T. B. "Mother-Infant Interaction Among the Gusii of Kenya." In T. M. Field, A. M. Sostek, P. Vietze, and P. H. Leiderman (eds.), *Culture and Early Interactions*. Hillsdale, N.J.: Erlbaum, 1981.
Dunn, J. "Sibling Relationships in Early Childhood." *Child Development*, 1983, *54*, 787–811.
Dunn, J., and Kendrick, C. *Siblings: Love, Envy, and Understanding*. Cambridge, Mass.: Harvard University Press, 1982.
Gallagher, S. S., Guyer, B., Kotelchuck, M., Bass, J., Lovejoy, F. H., McLoughlin, E., and Mehta, K. "A Strategy for the Reduction of Childhood Injuries in Massachusetts: SCIPP." *New England Journal of Medicine*, 1982, *307* (16), 1015–1019.
Lamb, M. (ed.). *The Father's Role: Cross-Cultural Perspectives*. Hillsdale, N.J.: Erlbaum, 1987.
LeVine, R. A. "Parental Goals: A Cross-Cultural View." *Teachers College Record*, 1974, *76* (2), 226–239.
LeVine, R. A. "Childrearing as Cultural Adaptation." In P. H. Leiderman, S. R. Tulkin, and A. Rosenfeld (eds.), *Culture and Infancy: Variations in the Human Experience*. New York: Academic Press, 1977.
LeVine, S. E. "Childhood Behavior Disorders in a Gusii Community in Southwestern Kenya." Paper presented at the meeting of the Society for Research in Child Development, Boston, April 3, 1981.
Super, C. M., and Harkness, S. "The Infant's Niche in Rural Kenya and Metropolitan America." In L. L. Adler (ed.), *Cross-Cultural Research at Issue*. New York: Academic Press, 1981.
U.S. Department of Labor. *Childcare: A Workforce Issue*. Report of the Secretary's Task Force, U.S. Department of Labor. Washington, D.C.: U.S. Government Printing Office, April 1988.

Whiting, J. "Environmental Constraints on Infant Care Practices." In R. H. Munroe, R. L. Munroe, and B. B. Whiting (eds.), *Handbook of Cross-Cultural Human Development.* New York: Garland, 1981.

Amy L. Richman is a research associate in education at the Harvard Graduate School of Education and director of research at Work/Family Directions, a Boston management and consulting firm specializing in work and family matters.

Patrice M. Miller is completing her doctoral work at the Harvard Graduate School of Education and is an instructor in psychology at the University of Massachusetts–Boston.

Margaret Johnson Solomon is completing her doctoral work at the Harvard Graduate School of Education on the effect of network patterns on parental goals, beliefs, and childcare.

Swedish parents view pregnancy and early infancy as a time of great vulnerability despite the fact that Sweden has a very low infant mortality rate.

Parenthood and Infancy in Sweden

Barbara Welles-Nystrom

This chapter explores the experience of parenthood and infant care in Sweden, particularly the features that distinguish it from parental experience elsewhere. The Swedish case is examined as an urban-industrial society with low fertility and infant mortality rates as well as extensive health and welfare services in support of reproduction. Sweden is at the low end on the global continuum of reproductive rates, with only six infant deaths per 1,000 live births and a total fertility rate of 1.6 births per woman, and it has had very low fertility and infant mortality rates for more than fifty years. Sweden's first-time mothers are among the world's oldest, averaging 26.4 years of age, since most Swedish women begin their occupational careers before their reproductive lives. The majority (65 percent) of mothers with young children are employed at least half-time (SCB, 1981).

The government provides benefits to encourage women to bear more children, including a parental insurance program that covers

This research was partly funded by a grant from the American Scandinavian Foundation. The author also gratefully acknowledges the assistance of Jan Winberg, Peter de Chateau, and John Lind, all of the Karolinska Hospital in Stockholm, and the mothers, fathers, and infants who participated in this study.

R. A. LeVine, P. M. Miller, and M. M. West (eds.). *Parental Behavior in Diverse Societies.*
New Directions for Child Development, no. 40. San Francisco: Jossey-Bass, Summer 1988.

mother and child through pregnancy, childbirth, and infancy. It subsidizes one parent for a nine-month period at 90 percent of salary to take care of the newborn child. Another nine months of childcare leave is allowed at a reduced rate of salary, and a further eighteen-month period with no reimbursement. The parent's job or one of equal responsibility must be kept available for her or his return to work at any time during this three years of leave permitted after the child's birth. All parents of preschool children are legally entitled to work less than full time and cannot be penalized for doing so. Sick benefits include sixty days per child annually for one parent at the guaranteed benefit rate of 90 percent salary.

These family policies are frequently revised (especially during election years) to improve conditions for the parents of young children. Although originally designed to encourage more births, they are increasingly justified in terms of parental well-being and child development. Swedish government policy anticipates parental concerns regarding the emotional, medical, and developmental needs of infants, at least for the first nine months of life, which is regarded as a vulnerable period particularly for socioemotional development.

My research on parental goals and infant care was carried out in Sweden during 1980–1982, as an extension of a study on the effects of maternal age and transition to parenthood (Welles, 1982; Welles-Nystrom and DeChateau, 1987). I have since had the experience of being married to a Swede, of giving birth to two children in Sweden, and of working there. This chapter is written for a U.S. readership. If I misrepresent Swedish culture, I do so as an anthropologist who, even after years of residence and participation in the country, is also somewhat of an outsider.

My main point in this chapter concerns a paradox that faces any model of human parenthood—namely, that Swedish parents are concerned with the viability and vulnerability of their offspring in spite of the extremely low risk to infant survival indicated by Sweden's infant mortality rate. Indeed, these parents may be more concerned and manifestly anxious about health risks than are parents in sub-Saharan Africa and other places where the risks to infant survival are twenty-five times as high. Understanding this phenomenon requires attention to the context in which Swedes become parents and care for infants.

Contexts of Pregnancy and Infant Care

Swedish medical opinion, widely disseminated through the mass media, portrays the pregnant woman and the fetus as vulnerable and advises her to assure the survival of the baby through maternal health clinics run by midwives who are occasionally assisted by gynecologists.

Mothers-to-be are advised on diet and health so that the fetus will grow and develop properly. The vulnerability of the child during pregnancy and the birth process is considered to last into the postpartum period for at least the first nine months of life. Parents accept the belief that they should care for their infants themselves during the first nine months in order to facilitate parent-offspring bonding and to establish a relationship that will balance the government-organized daycare that most Swedish children go into later on. The parental insurance program is seen as facilitating this relationship during its most vulnerable period.

Responsibility for infant care is vested in both parents. Fathers are expected to be actively involved in the care of their babies and even to become primary caretakers when mothers return to work. Public opinion favors the idea that men can be as nurturant as women, and an increasing number of infants are in fact being cared for by their fathers—a noteworthy departure for a human population.

Data Collection

The main source of data for this chapter is a developmental and ethnographic study I conducted at the Karolinska Hospital in Stockholm during 1980–1982 on the experiences of fifty-three primiparous mothers aged twenty to forty years and their infants. The first stage of data collection began in the eighth month of pregnancy and ended four months after birth. Research methods included semistructured interviews about the transition to motherhood as well as questionnaires regarding the division of labor in the household, child care, and norms of maternal behavior. These instruments were administered during pregnancy, the perinatal period, and when the infant was four months old.

The second stage of data collection occurred at ten months. The first twenty mothers who participated in the study were recontacted for further interviewing about parental goals and infant care and a two-hour naturalistic observation. In the analysis, the women aged twenty to twenty-nine years were compared with those aged thirty to thirty-nine to reveal differences in experience and development specific to each cohort.

Maternal Beliefs and Attitudes

The interviews with pregnant women revealed that, although they were aware of the low infant mortality rate in Sweden, they were not without concerns about the survival of their own offspring. They and other expectant parents they knew did not purchase anything in advance for the infant, believing that to do so would tempt fate. If "anything should happen" to the baby, the women said, they would not want to have reminders of it left behind.

A majority of mothers in both age cohorts, when interviewed ten months after giving birth, emphasized feeding as something a mother could do to assure the health of her infant, but breast-feeding was mentioned by a majority only among the older mothers. In the first stage of the data collection, however, all fifty-three of the pregnant women had said they expected to breast-feed their babies. After birth, it was the older women who experienced more difficulties with breast-feeding. Results from the Broussard Neonatal Perception Inventory (NPI) showed that the older mothers had lower expectations of the average baby's nursing ability ($\chi^2 = 5.62$, $p < 0.02$), a lower perception of their own infant's nursing behavior ($\chi^2 = 4.96$, $p < 0.05$), and more reported problems with nursing ($\chi^2 = 4.2$, $p < 0.05$). They also stayed longer in the hospital after birth ($\chi^2 = 4.4$, $p < 0.05$), which usually reflects a lengthier attempt to establish breast-feeding. While we do not have the data to tell whether the older mothers actually had more trouble with breast-feeding, it is clear that a larger proportion of them viewed it as problematic, while apparently considering it a high priority for child health. One thirty-three-year-old mother said she saw breast-feeding as "a test to be passed," believing that it was nutritionally, psychologically, and biologically the best way to feed her child. Thus, for at least some of the older women, there was a discrepancy between their standards of maternal behavior and what they considered or experienced to be possible for them as mothers.

The sample mothers recognized that infants have needs for playful interaction and cognitive stimulation as well as for loving nurturance through breast-feeding, though this was not spontaneously mentioned by the majority of women interviewed. Furthermore, some complained that their ten-month-old babies were too demanding of social attention, a tendency called *salskapssjuka*, meaning literally "sick for company." Some babies were called *mammig*, which means that the child not only prefers mother to another adult but will refuse to do anything with another member of the family. Mothers recognized that the infant's demands were in conflict with their own need for autonomy, and they said they must try to take the baby's perspective and understand the demand for attention as part of normal development. Here there seems to be a tension, at least for some mothers, between public definitions of what an infant needs and the mother's personal preferences.

Father's Involvement in Infant Care

Of the fifty-three women, forty-nine were living with the fathers of their infants, but only 10 percent were equally sharing parental leave—that is, were acting as primary caretaker for the baby for equal amounts of time ranging from four to six months. Another 27 percent of the fathers spent some time as primary caretaker, while the majority of fathers (63 percent) spent no extended time in full care of the infant.

While other research in Sweden (SCB, 1981) shows that the ideal of equality in the division of household tasks between husband and wife is realized more before the birth of the child than afterward, my study showed that feeding the infant by bottle and spoon was being redefined as a paternal task, one that let the father share the emotional satisfaction of nurturing a baby. This sample may not be representative of the Swedish population as a whole, but it revealed some interesting differences between the age cohorts of primiparous mothers. In the younger cohort, mothers and their mates more frequently shared household tasks during pregnancy on an equal basis, doing them together or in rotation, while the older women and their mates more often divided the tasks according to their skills, such as she being responsible for the cooking and he for the cleaning. This continued after the child was born, when the younger parents tended to share all the tasks such as bathing the baby, while the older parents divided the tasks—for example, she feeding the baby and he putting it to bed. The younger mothers tended to say that their mates were "always confident" in caring for the infant, but the older women said their mates were confident "most of the time" (χ^2 = 12.0, $p < 0.001$), although the majority of both cohorts of fathers said they "always" felt confident.

The more "androgynous" division of infant care in the younger cohort can be attributed in part to the influence of government policy. The law granting fathers the right to parental leave took effect in 1973, when women in the older cohort were already between twenty-two and thirty-two years of age, while the younger women were mostly in their teens. The latter (and their mates) came to maturity at a time when it was beginning to seem more natural for men to care for babies. As one of the younger mothers said, "It's a matter of training. It took me three days to learn to change diapers. Since he's not home all the time, it might take him a little longer. Maybe five days." These mothers and their mates represent the direction of change in the care of infants in Sweden today, a change in parental attitudes and behavior heavily influenced by legislation.

Models of Parenting in Sweden

In Sweden more than most countries, urban parents look to medical science and a progressive government for guidance in matters of reproduction and child care. Newspapers and magazines provide the latest scientific information and social enlightenment to an educated public ready to apply it in their personal lives. One consequence of this may be that mothers become keenly aware of low-probability risks to pregnancy and childbirth, particularly in connection with delayed childbearing, so that these risks are more salient to them than is the low infant mortality rate. Thus, they may be more anxious about giving birth than their

80

counterparts in countries where the survival risks are much greater. By the same token, they measure their "performance" as mothers against optimal standards provided by medical experts in the press and through official health information; if breast-feeding is defined as optimal, older first-time mothers worry about whether they are capable of doing it effectively. They are serious about being modern mothers and giving their babies the best care possible, but the height of their aspirations, even with free government services, may deprive of them the security that folk models afford the mothers in more traditional societies.

The same responsiveness to new information and willingness to try new ways, however, can be a benefit to Swedish women as they manage the strenuous combination of childbearing and full-time work. With the government providing incentives for men to participate in child care, Swedish families are changing to a more balanced and adaptive distribution of domestic work. In this as in many other ways, the patterns of reproduction and child care in Sweden deserve close attention in the comparative study of human parenthood.

References

SCB (Statistiska Centralbyran). *Few Children—Birthrate Development, 1960–1978.* Stockholm, Sweden: Statistiska Centralbyran, 1981.
Welles, B. "Maternal Age and First Birth in Sweden: A Life Course Study." Unpublished doctoral thesis, Harvard Graduate School of Education, 1982.
Welles-Nystrom, B., and DeChateau, P. "Maternal Age and Transition to Motherhood: Prenatal and Perinatal Assessments." *Acta Psychiatrika Scandinavika,* 1987, *76,* 719–725.

Barbara Welles-Nystrom is head of the Behavioral Sciences Research Department, Stockholm College of Nursing, in Stockholm, Sweden. Her research concerns reproductive behavior in cross-cultural perspective, including the transition to motherhood, women's sense of self, and women's relationships with others.

Comparison of observed maternal behavior to infants in five cultures shows differences between agrarian and urban-industrial societies as well as culture-specific patterns related to each local context.

Maternal Behavior to Infants in Five Cultures

Amy L. Richman, Robert A. LeVine,
Rebecca Staples New, Gail A. Howrigan,
Barbara Welles-Nystrom, Sarah E. LeVine

In this chapter we compare the behavior of mothers to their own infants at three to four and nine to ten months of age in five of the societies described in the previous chapters—namely the Gusii of Kenya, Yucatec Mayan of Mexico, Italian, Swedish, and suburban Bostonian. Mothers and infants were observed naturalistically at home. To explain the differences in frequencies of maternal behavior, we examine the demographic, socioeconomic, and cultural contexts of infant care in these societies, asking: Is maternal behavior adaptive, and if so, to which aspects of the environment?

Previous Research

During the last decade, several observational studies comparing mother-infant interaction in culturally diverse samples have been published (Leiderman, Tulkin, and Rosenfeld, 1977; Field, Sostek, Vietze,

---

The research reported here was supported by the National Science Foundation, the Spencer Foundation, and the International Fertility Determinants Awards Program of the Population Council (subordinate contract number CP81.61A).

R. A. LeVine, P. M. Miller, and M. M. West (eds.). *Parental Behavior in Diverse Societies.*
New Directions for Child Development, no. 40. San Francisco: Jossey-Bass, Summer 1988.

and Leiderman, 1981; Super and Harkness, 1982). The body of evidence resulting from these studies is fragmentary because the samples tend to be small, the range of infant ages limited (usually to the three- to four-month period) and both the data collection methods (home or laboratory observations) and analytic categories variable from one study to another. It is nevertheless possible to draw some preliminary conclusions:

1. Most studies report significant cross-cultural differences in maternal behavior at three to four months or throughout the first year of life. The comparisons include Kalahari San foragers, Guatemalans, and Bostonians of two social classes (Konner, 1977); Navahos versus Anglos in New Mexico (Chisholm, 1981, 1983; Callaghan, 1981); Kipsigis of Kenya versus middle-class Americans (Super and Harkness, 1982); Yugoslavs versus Americans (Lewis and Ban, 1977); and Cubans, Puerto Ricans, South Americans, and U.S. blacks living in the same section of Miami (Field and Widmayer, 1981).

2. The most often reported dimensions of difference involve communicative behavior, specifically verbal communication. In other words, mothers of some cultures spend a greater proportion of their time talking to the babies, with longer utterances and/or longer bouts of verbal interaction. The differences are large. Significant differences in maternal speaking are reported even when mean frequencies in other behaviors such as face-to-face position or mutual gaze do not differ and even where economic factors are controlled.

3. Some culturally defined groups such as middle-class Anglo-Americans, are repeatedly found to engage in more talking to babies, while others, such as Navahos and U.S. blacks of lower socioeconomic status (SES), are repeatedly found to talk less.

4. Maternal talking to babies is usually correlated with socioeconomic status within U.S. samples (Feiring and Lewis, 1981), but cross-cultural variations in this behavior taken as a whole do not conform to simple contrasts between "advanced" and "backward" peoples based on levels of education, literacy, or technological development. For example, the Kalahari San foragers, a hunting and gathering people of Botswana, engage in reciprocal vocalization with their infants at about the same frequency as "lower-class" urban white Americans and much more frequently than agrarian Guatemalan villagers (Konner, 1977). Within the United States, low-SES Cubans talk more to their babies than low-SES Puerto Ricans (Field and Widmayer, 1981).

This last finding, insofar as it indicates that frequency of talking to babies is not always a reflection of maternal education, suggests that it may reflect cultural variations in speech norms and in the beliefs that determine their application to infants. In some cultures, it may be considered appropriate to talk to babies, in others not, and this would help account for the large differences in frequencies across groups.

Ethnographic findings support and elaborate this hypothesis. Ochs and Schieffelin (1984) report that Kaluli mothers in Papua New Guinea believe infants are not appropriate partners for verbal communication and rarely engage infants in dyadic verbal interactions prior to their acquisition of real words. Once the infant produces certain key words, however, Kaluli mothers engage in elaborate teaching routines, most often in triadic interactions with siblings. In contrast, the Kwara'ae of Malaita in the Solomon Islands believe that infants can understand adult speech long before they can produce words (Watson-Gegeo and Gegeo, 1986). Since skill in communication and in interaction are highly valued, Kwara'ae engage in direct language teaching through "calling out and repeating routines" begun at six months of age for the express purpose of accelerating the child's language acquisition. Thus, these two Melanesian cultures differ in beliefs concerning the linguistic educability of infants and in the apparent frequency with which mothers talk to their infants. This contrast suggests that quantitative variations in maternal speaking across cultures reflect cultural models of verbal interaction during infancy. Investigation of this possibility requires observation of mothers when their infants are older than the three- to four-month period in which so many cross-cultural studies have been conducted, since the child's ability to acquire communicative skills accelerates later in the first year.

We are specifically interested in the possibility that maternal talking to infants reflects a model of infant care differing in its premises from one in which infant care is defined primarily as nurturance and protection, with communication focused on physical response to the infant cry (Chapters One and Three). Mothers who speak infrequently to their infants are nevertheless caring for them, in accordance with a set of priorities that might reflect perceived risks to infant survival.

Methods

Observations of mother-infant interaction were conducted in five samples: twelve families from a Gusii community in rural Kenya, fourteen Mayan families from a town in Yucatán, twenty families from a town in central Italy, twenty families living in Stockholm, Sweden, and ten families from suburban Boston. In each community, women were contacted in the last months of pregnancy or shortly after giving birth and invited to participate in a comparative study of child development and parenthood. These families were recruited through health care providers or through birth records in the various communities. All infants who met crude criteria concerning health, gestational age, and developmental maturity, and whose families fell within the normal range of socially acceptable family organization within each culture were included

Table 1. Demographic Characteristics of the Five Samples

		Maternal Age	Maternal Education	Number of Children
Kenya	Mean	29.2	2.9	4.3
	SD	6.4	3.3	2.4
	Range	20–40	0–10	1–10
Mexico		23.8	2.5	3.6
		9.2	1.9	3.3
		14–41	0–6	1–10
Italy		28.1	7.3	2.2
		4.3	3.8	0.4
		21–36	5–16	2–3
United States		31.4	14.0	2.6
		3.2	2.2	0.7
		27–38	9–18	2–4
Sweden		28.7	12[a]	1.0
		4.6		0
		21–40		

[a] Complete information on educational level of Swedish mothers not available; however, each had at least twelve years of education and only one child.

in the sample. In each sample there were equal numbers of males and females. Table 1 presents demographic information on the samples.

Naturalistic observations of mother-infant interaction were carried out when the infant was three to four months old and/or nine to ten months old at the home of each sample child in the five communities. At each age point, several hourlong infant-centered observations were made from which a continuous record of behavior was produced that captured not only the frequency but also the sequence and context of social interaction.

Observations in the Gusii sample were made using a longhand narrative method in which the observer recorded each interactive behavior by mother and infant and noted the time at one-minute intervals. In subsequent coding of these observations, approximately fifty categories of interactive behavior were developed; these formed the basis for the observational instrument used among the Mayans of Yucatán where, however, time was noted in thirty-second intervals. Observations in the Boston and Italian samples were collected with the Micro-Processing Observation Recording Equipment (MORE). The same observational instrument was used in both studies, and it utilized coding categories derived from the Gusii study so that comparable data would be generated. The MORE enables event-level recording with the added feature of marking, in this case, five-second time intervals as they occur. The Swedish observations used the coding categories from the Gusii study and imposed a ten-second interval. Although observational methods differed among samples, event-level data were collected on specified mother and infant behaviors in each study.

In addition to the behavior observations, we administered mother interviews as well as ethnographic interviews and observations in order to gather information on maternal beliefs about infant development, goals for socialization during the first two years of life, and infant care practices.

Results

Cross-cultural comparisons were made of the observational data on mother-infant interaction at the two age points. Table 2 presents data from the Gusii, Yucatec Mayan, and United States samples at three to four months, and Table 3 presents data from the Gusii, U.S., Italian, and Swedish samples at nine to ten months. Data on the following maternal behavior categories are compared across the groups: hold, talk, look, physical contact, and feed. In addition, we examined maternal responsiveness to infant crying and to nondistress vocalizations and reciprocal looking between mothers and infants. To adjust for differences in the sampling of behavior, we have expressed the occurrence of specific categories of maternal behavior as proportions of total maternal behavior during the observation period; this technique is similar to that used by Lewis and Ban (1977) in their five-culture comparison.

Maternal Behavior with Three- to Four-Month-Olds. Within-group comparison of the Gusii, Mayan, and U.S. maternal behaviors at infant age three to four months indicates high intraculture consistency using Kendall's coefficient of concordance (w = 0.46, 0.90, and 0.83; $p < 0.01$ for all). Table 2 shows maternal behavior across the three groups to be invariant only in that there is some behavior in every category in each group and that holding is the most frequent behavior for all. The samples diverge in the rank ordering of maternal behaviors, suggesting different patterns and contexts of infant care. The Gusii pattern is characterized by frequent holding and physical contact but infrequent verbal and visual interaction. In contrast, the profile for the U.S. sample features visual and verbal behaviors; infants were held in little more than half of the interactions with the mother. The Yucatec Mayan pattern is in some respects intermediate between the Gusii and U.S., consisting of frequent holding, feeding, and visual interaction but infrequent verbal interaction. The coefficient of concordance across the three groups is 0.62 (n.s.) (nonsignificant).

In addition to indicating the relative frequencies of maternal behavior, these figures are informative about the organization of maternal

86

Table 2. Mean Proportion of Total Maternal Behavior in Five
Cultures—Maternal Behavior at Infant Age Three to Four Months

	Kenyan Gusii (n = 9)		Yucatec Mayan (n = 13)		U.S. (n = 9)	
	Mean	SD	Mean	SD	Mean	SD
Hold	1.00	.17	.90	.08	.54	.16
Talk	.11	.08	.19	.08	.25	.08
Look	.12	.06	.52	.11	.40	.17
Physical Contact	.26	.13	.65	.14	.20	.07
Feed	.08	.05	.30	.14	.04	.06

Table 3. Mean Proportion of Total Maternal Behavior in Five
Cultures—Maternal Behavior at Infant Age Nine to Ten Months

	Kenyan Gusii (n = 17)		Italian (n = 20)		U.S. (n = 9)		Sweden (n = 20)	
	Mean	SD	Mean	SD	Mean	SD	Mean	SD
Hold	.88	.51	.26	.24	.25	.09	.10	.19
Talk	.14	.08	.39	.13	.29	.07	.68	.28
Look	.12	.06	.78	.13	.43	.19	.32	.13
Physical Contact	.28	.17	.19	.08	.10	.07	.17	.08
Feed	.04	.05	.06	.05	.05	.06	.01	.02

behavior. Since the individual behaviors are expressed as proportions of mothers' overall behavior totals, further distinction emerges between the Gusii and Yucatecan patterns as opposed to that of the U.S. mothers. In both the Gusii and Yucatec Mayan samples, mothers held their infants in in holding between the Gusii and Yucatec Mayan mothers on the one hand, and the U.S. mothers on the other, T-tests performed on the proportion scores, shown in Table 4, yield significant differences between in only half of the U.S. mothers' interactions with their three- to four-month-olds; they often looked at and talked to their infants from a distance. Analysis of infant's position during interaction in this Boston sample shows that four-month-old infants spend approximately 25 percent of awake time in baby equipment such as infant seats or swings. In the U.S. sample, then, communicative behaviors by the mother frequently occur not while the infant is being lulled and quieted in the mother's arms but when they are not in physical contact.

High proportions of holding in the Gusii and Yucatecan samples reflect the importance of soothing and comforting among infant care practices in both groups. The question of whether holding actually operates to soothe and comfort at this age cannot be examined in the Gusii and Yucatecan data because the infants are being held almost all the time. In the U.S. sample, however, where holding occurred in approximately 40 percent of the total observations, it was possible to examine the relationship between the occurrence of holding and subsequent infant behaviors. Using lag sequential analyses (Gottman and Bakeman, 1978), we calculated the conditional probability of occurrence of certain infant behaviors following holding based on their simple probabilities of occurrence. We compared these predicted values to the actual observed values of certain infant behaviors, when the mother was holding the infant. Maternal holding served to decrease the likelihood of subsequent infant crying ($p<0.05$), looking (n.s.), and nondistress vocalization ($p<0.01$).

That maternal holding in the U.S. sample seems to "dampen" or inhibit infant behavior may explain why, in the Gusii and Yucatec samples, where three- and four-month-old infants are held most of their waking hours, the mean frequencies of crying per four hours of observation are 81 (Gusii) and 73 (Yucatán) as compared with 190 in the U.S. sample. The consequence of less holding for the U.S. infants seem to be more crying and vocalizing than the Gusii and Yucatec infants. In other words, the Gusii and Yucatec mothers use a caretaking style that apparently produces a quieter, calmer infant, while the U.S. mothers have a maternal style that does not inhibit infant distress or nondistress vocalizations.

Pairwise comparisons of the rank ordering of maternal behavior across the three groups yields the following Spearman correlation coefficients: Gusii-Yucatec, $r = 0.83$ (n.s.); Gusii-U.S., $r = 0.68$ (n.s.); and Yucatec-U.S., $r = 0.45$ (n.s.). Although the positive correlations tap a certain degree of invariance, these results indicate no significant similarity across the three groups at this age. Aside from the substantial differences in holding between the Gusii and Yucatec Mayan mothers on the one hand, and the U.S. mothers on the other, t-tests performed on the proportion scores, shown in Table 4, yield significant differences between the Gusii and Mayan mothers on the relative frequencies of the four other maternal behaviors and significant differences between the U.S. and Gusii mothers on both verbal and visual interaction.

A third area of evidence for cultural diversity in mother-infant interaction at this age is visual attention by infants and mothers. We compared the mean number of intervals in which looking at mother by infant or looking at infant by mother occurred at three to four months in each sample. U.S. and Yucatecan mothers do much more visual monitoring of their infants than the infants do of their mothers: In the U.S. sample, looking occurred in 26 percent of the intervals by mothers compared with 8 percent of the intervals by infants; in the Yucatec Mayan sample, looking occurred in 34 percent of the intervals by mothers and 15 percent of the intervals by infants. Gusii mothers, however, do not look at their infants much more than the latter look at them; looking occurred in 6 percent of the intervals by mothers compared with 5 percent of the intervals by infants.

Maternal Behavior with Nine- to Ten-Month-Olds. The profiles of maternal behavior with nine- to ten-month-old infants in the Gusii, Italian, U.S., and Swedish samples also show cultural variations (Table 3). As at three to four months, there is high within-group consistency in maternal behavior for each sample. Kendall's coefficients of concordance are as follows: Gusii, $w = 0.57$; Italian, $w = 0.73$; U.S., $w = 0.75$; and Swedish, $w = 0.88$; all are significant ($p < 0.01$). When comparisons across the four samples are made, two distinctive patterns emerge: The Gusii mothers exhibit a pattern of maternal care that is very similar to their pattern at three to four months characterized by frequent holding and physical contact with low amounts of verbal and visual interaction. In contrast, the maternal style in the U.S. sample and the two European samples emphasize more distal behaviors—visual and verbal interaction with less frequent physical contact. This difference between the Gusii maternal pattern on the one hand and the Boston, and European patterns on the other is further supported by Spearman rank-order correlations performed on all pairs of the four samples. The Gusii rank ordering of behaviors was correlated at 0.10 with each of the others, whereas the U.S., Italian, and Swedish profiles were correlated at 0.80 or higher with each other. (Only the U.S.-Italian correlation, 1.00, was significant).

The relative decline of physical contact and increase in distal forms of maternal behavior represent a shift in the U.S. sample after three to four months: t-tests for correlated samples yield a significant decrease in holding from the first to the second age point ($t = 3.62$, $p < 0.01$). The contrast in patterns between the Gusii, on the one hand, and the U.S., Italian, and Swedish mothers, on the other, is especially noteworthy in terms of the infant's developing motor, cognitive, and communicative abilities, as documented in the behavior observations. By nine to ten months, the infants in each sample were sitting up without support and in most cases crawling; this means they were capable of supporting themselves without maternal intervention or assistance. In addition, their fine motor and cognitive skills had progressed to such a point that they were able to manipulate objects such as toys, clothing, and solid foods. They had also acquired rudimentary social and communicative skills; through gestures and vocalizations they conveyed messages to their caregivers. In spite of these developmental changes, Gusii mothers continued to focus their infant care on soothing and quieting, using a pattern of maternal behaviors begun in the early months of life. The continued position of holding as the most frequent maternal behavior at

Table 4. Comparison of Maternal Behavior to Infants Three to Four Months Old, Expressed in Proportion Scores

Maternal Behavior	Gusii (n = 9)	Yucatec (n = 13)	t	Gusii (n = 9)	Boston (n = 9)	t	Yucatec (n = 13)	Boston (n = 9)	t
Hold	1.00	.90	1.87	1.00	.54	5.96[b]	.90	.54	7.06[b]
Talk	.11	.19	2.31[a]	.11	.25	4.24[b]	.19	.25	1.74
Look	.12	.52	10.34[b]	.12	.40	4.67[b]	.52	.40	2.03
Physical Contact	.26	.65	6.67[b]	.26	.20	1.22	.65	.20	8.94[b]
Feed	.08	.30	4.53[b]	.08	.04	1.54	.30	.04	5.26[b]

[a] $p < 0.05$
[b] $p < 0.01$

Table 5. Mean Percent of Intervals in Which Mother-Infant Looking
Occurred, at Nine to Ten Months

	Mothers Looking at Infants	Infants Looking at Mothers
Gusii	9	9
U.S.	28	8
Italy	40	23
Sweden	32	23

a time when the infant is capable of sitting alone suggests that the Gusii mother's behavior reflects a preference for physical contact that does not depend on the infant's motor development. In contrast, the use of physical contact in the U.S. sample seems to be attuned to motor development because it decreases in relative frequency with the child's age and improving motor abilities. Holding of nine- to ten-month-olds occurs on the average in 28 percent of the intervals of observation in the Gusii sample, 17 percent of the intervals in the American sample, 14 percent of the intervals in the Italian sample, and 10 percent of the intervals in the Swedish sample.

The data on maternal responsiveness to crying from three of the samples (Gusii, Italian, and U.S.) are consistent with this picture. In the Gusii sample, mothers tend to use holding or physical contact to comfort their nine- and ten-month-old infants, while in the Italian and U.S. samples mothers relied on distal behaviors—looking or talking to soothe their babies. In the U.S. sample, for example, maternal talking as a response to the infant's cry is significantly more frequent than would have been predicted from the base rate of talking (using the method of comparing predicted and observed probabilities cited earlier, $p < 0.03$). This is in contrast to the earlier age point at which U.S. as well as Gusii mothers used holding or physical contact as their most frequent response to crying.

Finally, comparisons of looking behavior between mothers and infants again indicate the divergence in mother-infant interaction between the Gusii sample and the U.S. and European samples. Using the mean number of intervals in which looking occurred, Table 5 gives the data for the four samples. As at the earlier age point, the Gusii case is the only one in which the mean frequency of looking is similar for mothers and infants; in the other samples, mothers gaze at their infants more frequently than infants gaze at their mothers.

Discussion

In comparing samples of Kenyan (Gusii) and United States (suburban Boston) mother-infant pairs with Yucatec Mayans when the infants were three to four months old and with Italians and Swedes at nine to ten months, we found differences in the mean frequencies of specific maternal behaviors and in the patterning of the behaviors at both age points. The evidence presented so far implies that, while there may be a universal repertoire of potential maternal responses to infants during the first year of life, mothers of different cultures either define the tasks of infant care differently or carry them out under such different conditions that their communicative behavior (response to crying, mutual gaze, talking) and the interactive experience of their infants are correspondingly divergent. This divergence is even more evident at ten months than it is at four, suggesting that cultural differences increase with infant development. We shall attempt to explain these cultural variations by examining the environmental contexts of maternal behavior to infants in each of the five samples.

The Gusii of Kenya. Three contextual features are important in interpreting the behavioral profile of Gusii mothers with their four- and ten-month-olds (shown in Tables 2 and 3): the high priorities of protection and soothing and the low priority of communicative exchange in their cultural model of infant care; the heavy work load of Gusii women and their lack of help and cooperation from other adults; and the emphasis on affective restraint in their conventional code of interpersonal communication, particularly between adult children and their parents.

Each of these features provides a basis for interpreting the behavioral profile. The Gusii interpret holding as a form of protection from physical hazards, including cooking fires and domestic animals, and they have no clear alternatives like playpens, infant seats, or cradleboards—or the hammocks used by Yucatec Mayans. This interpretation makes sense of why Gusii persist in holding babies at ten and, indeed, at fifteen months, after they are capable of locomotion. In the Gusii view, walking, though desirable as a developmental milestone, increases the risk that young children will hurt themselves and makes continued holding necessary. Soothing through rapid physical comforting when the baby cries is also seen by the Gusii as a means of keeping infants safe and healthy. Since, as we have suggested, such measures also keep babies quiet and more easily managed (at least so long as they are held on someone's body), this form of care may also be a way of reducing the mother's energy output, reflecting her heavy work load.

Holding and soothing, then (the two most frequent maternal behaviors shown in Tables 2 and 3), may serve to protect Gusii infants from harm and keep them calm. As suggested in the original formulation (LeVine, 1974), keeping a baby calm through consistently rapid comforting may make it easier for the mother to tell when the infant is becoming sick, as opposed to hungry or temporarily distressed, and may help her decide when special attention and efforts are required on her part. Such a strategy makes sense where infant mortality is frequent and could represent a historical adaptation of culturally constituted maternal behavior to high infant mortality rates. It is also convenient for overburdened mothers, who need clear indicators of when something more than routine is called for. Thus, this style of maternal behavior serves a number of functions for Gusii mothers and may well also be determined by its utilities in folk pediatrics and domestic management.

The low frequencies of looking and talking by Gusii mothers at both age points also reflect a number of culture-specific features: the expressed belief that babies are incapable of understanding verbal communication and that talking to babies is more appropriate for children than for mothers; the importance of gaze aversion in Gusii conventions of interpersonal communication, and particularly in the code of avoidance/affective restraint between parents and children; and, once again, the heavy work load that inclines Gusii mothers against time-consuming and energy-intensive forms of interaction with their offspring.

Although Gusii women are busy with domestic and agricultural tasks and the burden of total responsibility of the care, feeding, clothing, and school attendance of their numerous children, observations indicated that their time-energy budgets permit more looking at and talking to their babies than they actually do. Mothers were often observed breastfeeding for an extended period without ever looking down at the baby; at other times when visual monitoring was possible and when the baby was looking at the mother, mothers rarely returned the gaze. Thus, the work burden and time-energy budget do not constitute as plausible an explanation as one that includes the mother's preference for avoiding visual and verbal contact with the infant.

On the other hand, the mother's preference may be based on her concept of the consequences for her future time-energy expenditures of visual and verbal attention to the child during infancy. Some sample mothers complained that children sent to (maternal) grandmothers, particularly at the time of weaning, came back demanding too much attention from the mother at a time when her attention was turned to the next baby. They implicitly recognized that visual and verbal interaction with a young child builds up expectations that might interfere with work and infant care routines at a later time. Thus, the avoidance of looking and talking may be partly explained, not by current incompatibility with the maternal work schedule, but by a maternal theory of infant habituation that enables them to anticipate future time and energy demands.

That mothers prefer not to engage their infants in visual and verbal communication may also be attributable to the Gusii code of avoidance and gaze aversion. Gusii adults conversing with each other rarely look into each other's eyes; in fact, they usually stand or sit side by side or at right angles to one another when talking. To look into another's eyes at any time other than the moment of greeting is only a serious infraction of the rules; however, when one of the conversational partners is a real or classificatory parent of the other (that is, of the parents' generation), that is forbidden by the code of avoidance. Although this code does not explicitly apply to mothers with their infants and small children, it seems plausible that it might influence the mother in her contacts even with her young offspring—at least in situations where they can be observed—as an anticipation of their future relationship. Indeed, since grandmothers, particularly on the mother's side, are free of the avoidance code in interacting with their grandchildren at any age, this would help explain why mothers complain about the expectations children bring back from staying with them; grandmothers engage freely in the visual and verbal interaction from which mothers restrain themselves. We cannot prove this interpretation with quantitative data, but we hypothesize that the influence of the avoidance code combines with pragmatic anticipation of developing an excessively demanding child to explain why Gusii mothers so rarely look at and talk to their infants.

The Yucatec Mayans. The high frequencies of holding and physical contacts shown in Table 2 for Yucatec Mayan mothers reflect the strategy of soothing and the goal of a quiet baby that they share with the Gusii. That the Mayan babies at three to four months old are not being held all the time is due to a New World device not found in Africa—the hammock, which, when wrapped around a baby, can keep it safely contained from the hazards of the floor in a position conducive to sleep. The much greater frequencies of physical contact, looking, and feeding among the Yucatec Mayan mothers than among the Gusii indicates a greater concentration of undivided attention to the baby at this age. With a lighter work load and more help from other women, they are freer to provide this kind of attention, while the busy Gusii mothers are often performing other domestic tasks while caring for their babies. Finally, the Mayans do not have conventions of gaze aversion or parent-child avoidance that would inhibit their looking at and talking with their infants. They look at them a greater proportion of the time than the other two groups, though their talking is less frequent than in the U.S. sample.

The United States: Suburban Bostonians. The Boston mothers are relatively high in frequency of talking and looking at both age points, reflecting both the belief that infants can communicate socially and the value these mothers place on conversational interaction with their offspring. Holding, which is much less frequent than among the Gusii and Yucatec Mayans at the earlier age, declines drastically by the time the infant is nine to ten months old, reflecting the value U.S. mothers put on independence and separateness and the use they make of infant seats and playpens that contain infants without human physical contact.

The Italians. The Italian mothers contrast with the Gusii and Yucatecan mothers in that, although they want a clean, healthy baby, they expect early communicative development during infancy. They repeatedly mentioned proper feeding, hygiene, and protection from elements as essential to infant care and as incompatible with exploratory play. Infants are rarely left to crawl or sit on the tiled floors, which are cold during the winter months, and mothers prevent toddlers from engaging in any kind of outside activity that would result in soiled clothing or exposure to sun or cold. They believe in feeding on a regular schedule and are ready to use force-feeding if necessary to make sure that the child ingests a certain amount of food.

The Italian mothers reported that infants were able to recognize the mother's face and voice in the first months of life. The importance of the infant's sociability to the mother was evident in the frequent teaching of the hand gesture for the *ciao* greeting. It was often observed that a family member took the infant's hand to help her greet a visitor.

The Italian behavioral profile with ten-month-olds shown in Table 3 reflects the emphasis on communication, with looking and talking very frequent, more so than in the U.S. sample. Other differences between the Italian and U.S. mothers, though very striking to ethnographic observation (see Chapter Five), are not captured by this crude actuarial approach.

The Swedish. The behavioral profile of the Swedish mothers resembles that of the U.S. and Italians in that talking and looking are the most frequent categories with ten-month-olds, but their proportions are by far the highest on talking and considerably lower on looking. The greater frequency of talking seems to reflect the fact that their children are firstborns who can be given the mother's undivided attention, while the U.S. and Italian mothers have older children in the house to whom they are sometimes speaking even when taking care of the infant. The low proportion of looking in relation to talking may reflect the influence of Swedish norms of face-to-face communication or a generally low level of visual monitoring by mothers who expect their infants to explore a physical environment that is free of dangers.

Conclusion

In each of the five cases, we have been able to provide a plausible, if partial, explanation of the culture-specific profile of maternal behavior in terms of contextual features such as maternal beliefs and priorities, domestic organization, and technology and environmental risk. The evidence from these five cultures at two age points in the first year, then, indicates that there are cultural differences in maternal behavior and that they can be accounted for in terms of the particular socioeconomic and cultural environments in which children are being raised. A pattern of verbal and visual interaction is characteristic of the European and American samples, drawn from urban-industrial populations in which fertility and infant mortality rates are low and mothers attend school for many more years than they do in the agrarian settings of Kenya and Yucatán. Mothers in the Gusii and Mayan samples behave in accordance with cultural codes that assign a high priority to physical nurturance, soothing, and protection during the first months of life and tend to postpone communication as such until later; their infants are, as a consequence, quieter than those of the U.S. sample, whose active communication is encouraged by maternal talking and looking.

This divergence in priorities and goals for infant care does not mean that maternal behavior is homogeneous within the categories of urban-industrial and agrarian societies. On the contrary, we have seen here and in the extended portraits of the previous chapters that the preferences of Italian mothers for wide-ranging sociability and unilateral communication, as well as their emphasis on physical protection through heavy clothing and feeding, contrast sharply with the goals, strategies, and styles of the U.S. mothers. Some of the difference, particularly the relative emphasis on protection, may be attributed to the high infant mortality rate in Italy as recently as thirty years ago, but the rest seems to be due to differences in cultural conceptions of the person, the family, and interpersonal relationships prevailing in Italy and the United States.

Similarly, we found that, though the Gusii and Yucatec Mayans are both agrarian peoples with relatively high fertility and infant mortality rates (the Gusii considerably higher) and relatively low levels of maternal schooling, they do differ in some aspects of maternal behavior, particularly looking at the three-month-old baby, which Gusii mothers inhibit in accordance with a cultural code of parent-child avoidance but which is not inhibited by the Mayan mothers, who in any event have more leisure time with their babies due to the sharing of domestic work with other women in their compounds. Thus the long-standing demographic and socioeconomic contexts of populations are not translated directly into observable maternal behavior but are mediated through varying traditions of domestic organization and interpersonal behavior that diversify further the environments of child care.

This analysis suggests that more detailed studies of mothers' goals during infancy and early childhood, their strategies for pursuing them, and the cultural models that represent both would help to clarify the ways in which variations among human populations are translated into differing patterns of infant care.

References

Callaghan, J. "A Comparison of Anglo, Hopi, and Navajo Mothers and Infants." In T. Field, A. Sostek, P. Vietze, and P. H. Leiderman (eds.), *Culture and Early Interactions.* Hillsdale, N.J.: Erlbaum, 1981.

Chisholm, J. "Residence Patterns and the Environment of Mother-Infant Interaction Among the Navajo." In T. Field, A. Sostek, P. Vietze, and P. H. Leiderman (eds.), *Culture and Early Interactions.* Hillsdale, N.J.: Erlbaum, 1981.

Chisholm, J. *Navajo Infancy.* New York: Aldine, 1983.

Feiring, C., and Lewis, M. "Middle Class Differences in the Mother-Child Interaction and the Child's Cognitive Development." In T. Field, A. Sostek, P. Vietze, and P. H. Leiderman (eds.), *Culture and Early Interactions.* Hillsdale, N.J.: Erlbaum, 1981.

Field, T., Sostek, A., Vietze, P., and Leiderman, P. H. (eds.). *Culture and Early Interactions.* Hillsdale, N.J.: Erlbaum, 1981.

Field, T., and Widmayer, S. "Mother-Infant Interactions Among Lower SES Black, Cuban, Puerto Rican, and South American Immigrants." In T. Field, A. Sostek, P. Vietze, and P. H. Leiderman (eds.), *Culture and Early Interactions.* Hillsdale, N.J.: Erlbaum, 1981.

Gottman, J., and Bakeman, R. "The Sequential Analysis of Observational Data." In M. Lamb, S. Suomi, and G. Stephenson (eds.), *Methodological Problems in the Study of Social Interaction.* Madison: University of Wisconsin Press, 1978.

Konner, M. "Infancy Among the Kalahari Desert San." In P. H. Leiderman, S. R. Tulkin, and A. Rosenfeld (eds.), *Culture and Infancy.* New York: Academic Press, 1977.

Leiderman, P. H., Tulkin, S. R., and Rosenfeld, A. (eds.). *Culture and Infancy.* New York: Academic Press, 1977.

LeVine, R. A. "Parental Goals: A Cross-Cultural View." *Teachers College Record,* 1974, *76* (2), 226–239.

Lewis, M., and Ban, P. "Variance and Invariance in Mother-Infant Interaction: A Cross-Cultural Study." In P. H. Leiderman, S. R. Tulkin, and A. Rosenfeld (eds.), *Culture and Infancy.* New York: Academic Press, 1977.

Ochs, E., and Schieffelin, B. "Language Acquisition and Socialization: Three Developmental Stories." In R. Shweder and R. A. LeVine (eds.), *Culture Theory.* New York: Cambridge University Press, 1984.

Super, C. M., and Harkness, S. "The Development of Affect in Infancy and Early Childhood." In D. Wagner and H. Stevenson (eds.), *Cultural Perspectives on Child Development.* New York: Freeman, 1982.

Watson-Gegeo, K., and Gegeo, D. "Calling-Out and Repeating Routines in Kwara'ae Children's Language Socialization." In B. B. Schieffelin and E. Ochs (eds.), *Language Socialization Across Cultures,* Part I. New York: Cambridge University Press, 1986.

Amy L. Richman is a research associate in education at the Harvard Graduate School of Education and director of research at Work/Family Directions, a Boston management and consulting firm specializing in work and family matters.

Robert A. LeVine is Roy E. Larsen Professor of Education and Human Development at the Harvard Graduate School of Education and professor of anthropology at Harvard University.

Rebecca Staples New is assistant professor of child and family studies at the College for Human Development, Syracuse University.

Gail A. Howrigan is currently a full-time mother; she has conducted or participated in studies of mother-infant interaction and malnutrition in Yucatán.

Barbara Welles-Nystrom is head of the Behavioral Sciences Research Department, Stockholm College of Nursing, in Stockholm, Sweden.

Sarah E. LeVine is research associate in the Laboratory of Human Development at the Harvard Graduate School of Education.

*National sample data from eight countries are analyzed
to explore hypotheses about cross-cultural differences
in childrearing patterns.*

Cross-Cultural Differences in Childrearing Goals

Lois Wladis Hoffman

With this chapter the focus of this volume moves from infancy to childhood more generally and to the question of how cross-cultural differences
affect childrearing patterns across the stages of childhood. There are several different theories that have been proposed. LeVine (1974), for example, has hypothesized that differences in childrearing patterns evolved in
response to environmental risks threatening the child's survival and self-
maintenance. Melvin Kohn (1969) has put forth a theory to explain social
class differences but that is also applicable to cross-cultural differences—
namely, that occupational roles affect an adult's attitudes and values and
thus influence his or her role as parent. A related theory, discussed by
Barry, Bacon, and Child (1967); Barry, Child, and Bacon (1959); and Hoffman (1977, 1984, 1986), is that parents rear their children so as to encourage the development of those qualities and attitudes needed for their
expected adult roles, which differ from society to society. Super and Harkness (1982) see cross-cultural differences as resulting from the fact that
adult beliefs about the nature of children or about the world in general
differ from group to group, and these beliefs affect parenting behavior.

This chapter is an adaptation of a previously published paper (Hoffman,
1987).

R. A. LeVine, P. M. Miller, and M. M. West (eds.). *Parental Behavior in Diverse Societies.*
New Directions for Child Development, no. 40. San Francisco: Jossey-Bass, Summer 1988.

It is very difficult to choose a champion from among the various theories. Cross-cultural differences in childrearing orientations are multi-determined, and it may be that all of the processes operate to some extent. In this chapter, the aim is not to come up with a single theory but rather to use a particular data set for two purposes: to examine some of the predictions from two of the theories (LeVine's and Kohn's) for which the data are relevant and to propose an additional theory and explore its viability. The data to be examined are from the Cross-National Value of Children study.

The Cross-National Value of Children Study

The Cross-National Value of Children study was a cooperative research project conducted in 1975 involving investigators (F. Arnold, R. Bulatao, C. Buripakdi, B. Chung, R. K. Darroch, J. Fawcett, L. W. Hoffman, C. Kagitcibasi, S. J. Lee, Masri Singarimbun, T. H. Sun, and T. S. Wu) from eight countries: Indonesia, Korea, the Philippines, Singapore, Taiwan, Thailand, Turkey, and the United States. In each country, between 1,000 and 3,000 married women under forty were interviewed and at least one-quarter of their husbands. With the exception of Indonesia, each sample was nationally representative of that country. In Indonesia, the sample was limited to two ethnic groups, Javanese in Central Java and Sundanese in West Java. The study was concerned primarily with the psychological satisfactions that children are perceived to provide for their parents and the relationship between these and fertility attitudes and behavior.

LeVine's Theory

In an extension of his theory that childrearing patterns reflect the parents' concern for the child's survival, LeVine (1974) suggests that, where infant mortality is less but subsistence resources are scarce, parents will be preoccupied with the child's capacity for future economic self-maintenance. For example, many anthropologists (such as Barry, Child, and Bacon, 1959; Munroe and Munroe, 1972; Langman, 1973) have observed that obedience is a particularly valued trait in a child in agricultural economies, and LeVine suggests that this is because obedience is a necessary trait for surviving economically as an adult in rural societies. According to LeVine, this emphasis will be strongest when economic survival is in greatest jeopardy.

There are data relevant to this theory in the Cross-National Value of Children study. All of the respondents were asked, "What quality would you most like to see in your children at school age?" The answer was to be selected from a list of five qualities: to mind their parents (obedience); to be independent and self-reliant; to be popular; to do well in school; and to be a good person. Table 1 shows the wives' responses to this question, broken down by country and by rural-urban residence.

These data provide some support for LeVine's hypothesis. Of the three predominantly rural countries—Indonesia, Thailand, and the Philippines—two show an overwhelming endorsement of obedience as the most desired quality. In Indonesia, over 75 percent of the Javanese sample reported that the quality they most wanted to see in their children was "to mind." This response was also given by more than 64 percent of the Sundanese in Indonesia and more than 61 percent of the Philippine respondents. The one exception, Thailand, is much further than these two from a subsistence level. According to the United Nations (1982) figures for the corresponding time period, the per-capita calorie supply in Thailand is over subsistence levels while both the Philippines and Indonesia are under; furthermore, the per-capita protein supply in Thailand is fifty-two grams per day in contrast with forty-five for the Philippines and forty-three for Indonesia. Of all the countries in the Value of Children study, the Philippines and Indonesia are the lowest in per-capita calories and protein supply. Thus, the prediction that obedience will be most stressed in agricultural countries where subsistence resources are scarce is supported. On the other hand, it is interesting to note in Table 1 that, within a country, rural residence does not increase the tendency to select obedience as the most desired quality. Nor is it true, as LeVine's theory would imply, that the rural-urban difference is greater for the below-subsistence countries. The difference is no greater for Indonesia and the Philippines than it is for the United States.

Kohn's Theory

Tables 2 and 3 present data that bear on Kohn's hypothesis. Kohn and his colleagues (Kohn, 1963, 1969, 1980) have conducted their research in the United States and other industrialized countries. In these countries, where the father has a blue-collar occupation, the parents stress conformity to rules in their childrearing, whereas professional and managerial occupations lead parents to encourage initiative and independence. The parents value these traits because, in professional and managerial occupations, initiative and independence are believed to pay off, while, in blue-collar occupations, obedience and sticking to the rules are believed to pay off.

The data from the cross-national study are, in general, consistent with Kohn's hypothesis. Table 2 indicates the percentage of wives who chose obedience and independence as the most desired quality for school-age children, by father's occupation: professional and managerial, skilled and clerical, manual and service, or farm. Table 3 gives the husbands' responses. In all countries, except Indonesia for the wives and the United States for the husbands, parents in families where the husband is engaged in professional or managerial occupations were more likely than any other occupational category to say "independence" (all x^2 significant, $p < 0.05$). Where the husband is engaged in manual and service work, parents were more likely to say "to mind" although here the pattern is statistically significant ($p < 0.05$) only in the United States, Turkey, and Singapore.

The significance tests were two-tailed chi squares with one degree of freedom testing for each country: whether managerial and professional workers were more likely to say "independent" than all others; and whether manual workers were more likely to say "to mind" than were all others. (Throughout the chapter, only one level of significance is reported, $p < 0.05$, with $p < 0.10$ reported as approaching significance.)

The Value of Children to Parents and Childrearing Patterns

Hoffman and Hoffman (1973) developed a new theory to explain cross-cultural differences in childrearing in order to investigate fertility motivation (see Figure 1). At the core of this theory is the idea that children may satisfy certain basic needs for parents, such as the need for love, for fun and stimulation, or for economic security. Which needs children satisfy are affected by the social and economic structure of a particular society; thus, they differ for different groups. The needs that children satisfy, in turn, affect fertility and childrearing patterns.

A review of the literature (Hoffman and Hoffman, 1973) and subsequent research (Hoffman, 1980) have supported the idea that the various satisfactions of parenthood reported in a wide range of societies encompass the eight needs listed in Figure 1. In the cross-national study, all of the eight needs were indicated as needs children satisfy in each of the eight countries, but there was considerable variation in their prevalence in the different countries. Societies differ in how intensely each need is felt, in the extent to which children are seen as a possible source for satisfying the need, and in whether there are other sources for satisfying the need besides children.

For example, in the villages in India, poverty prevails and the need for economic security, particularly in old age when the parents can no longer work, is intensely felt. Sons are seen as a source of economic security, and their value is enhanced because there is no alternative. In this society, daughters belong to their husband's household and cannot help their parents. Overwhelmingly, the parents indicate that sons are valued for the economic security they can provide in old age (Poffenberger and Poffenberger, 1973). The particular value of sons in the Indian village leads not only to a wish for many children, since some will be girls and some will die before maturity, but it also leads to preferential treatment of sons over daughters and to instilling in sons a strong sense of loyalty to parents and of filial obligations.

Table 1. The Quality Mothers Would Most Like to See in Their Children (Percentage)

	Turkey	Indonesia (Javanese)	Indonesia (Sundanese)	Philippines	Thailand	Korea	Taiwan	Singapore	United States
To mind their parents									
Rural	38.6	73.3	66.9	61.3	26.6	17.0	28.5	20.4	18.4
Urban	34.1	77.5	63.9	65.2	30.7	11.6	15.6	31.6	14.5
To be independent and self-reliant									
Rural	4.1	2.4	7.2	5.8	4.7	35.1	13.2	45.0	25.3
Urban	13.1	8.6	13.4	4.0	18.0	60.5	27.7	37.2	25.0
To be popular with others									
Rural	4.7	2.1	1.3	1.2	2.5	6.7	7.4	0.9	2.6
Urban	7.6	0.5	2.5	0.3	3.0	3.6	8.7	1.9	2.5
To do well in school									
Rural	19.7	10.0	8.9	7.4	17.9	21.4	10.3	5.2	8.4
Urban	14.4	3.8	8.9	5.2	14.3	12.4	17.9	10.5	10.2
To be a good person									
Rural	33.0	12.2	15.8	24.3	47.4	19.9	40.6	28.4	45.3
Urban	30.7	9.5	11.4	25.3	34.0	11.9	30.1	18.7	47.8
n									
Rural	898	819	797	1,337	1,920	770	1,073	211	380
Urban	860	210	202	348	621	795	1,127	731	1,159

Source: Hoffman, 1987.

Table 2. Percentage of Wives Selecting Obedience and Independence as the Most Important Quality in Children, by Father's Occupation

	Professional	Skilled & Clerical	Manual & Service	Farm
Turkey				
To mind	26.0	36.9	39.6	37.9
To be independent	24.7	8.6	6.7	8.0
n	454	279	647	301
Indonesia (Javanese)				
To mind	79.3	69.7	76.5	73.7
To be independent	6.0	8.1	5.9	2.3
n	116	99	136	654
Indonesia (Sundanese)				
To mind	62.7	66.1	63.8	68.9
To be independent	12.0	12.1	9.7	3.6
n	209	224	207	331
Philippines				
To mind	58.2	58.7	63.8	61.7
To be independent	12.1	6.6	4.0	5.5
n	91	213	652	653
Thailand				
To mind	23.5	26.9	32.1	26.9
To be independent	29.2	20.4	10.0	3.2
n	243	323	711	1,205
Korea				
To mind	12.0	9.4	12.6	21.7
To be independent	67.6	65.0	51.1	24.3
n	142	426	499	350

Taiwan				
To mind	13.9	17.4	22.8	13.1
To be independent	31.4	26.4	17.9	10.5
n	510	288	892	447
Singapore				
To mind	17.9	24.8	33.8	16.0
To be independent	56.0	43.2	34.0	28.0
n	84	322	524	25
United States				
To mind	10.4	14.3	18.1	15.6
To be independent	29.1	28.6	21.9	24.4
n	498	133	744	45

Table 3. Percentage of Husbands Selecting Obedience and Independence as the Most Important Quality in Children, by Father's Occupation

	Professional	Skilled & Clerical	Manual & Service	Farm
Turkey				
To mind	20.4	34.1	43.0	37.2
To be independent	28.5	13.4	8.7	10.5
n	137	82	172	86
Indonesia (Javanese)				
To mind	50.0	58.3	74.0	70.5
To be independent	13.3	8.3	8.0	2.5
n	60	36	50	319
Indonesia (Sundanese)				
To mind	43.9	59.8	47.7	54.7
To be independent	14.9	12.4	11.4	7.1
n	114	97	88	170
Philippines				
To mind	63.2	60.0	60.1	62.4
To be independent	10.5	11.1	2.7	3.8
n	19	45	148	157
Thailand				
To mind	13.0	23.7	26.9	36.2
To be independent	37.0	27.8	19.3	5.4
n	92	97	212	311
Korea				
To mind	12.2	9.7	11.2	18.2
To be independent	82.9	75.0	61.5	33.1
n	41	124	143	121

Taiwan				
To mind	10.8	11.8	15.4	26.6
To be independent	35.1	34.7	25.8	11.8
n	279	127	384	203
Singapore				
To mind	12.2	16.0	23.0	5.9
To be independent	65.9	53.9	44.1	17.7
n	41	169	252	17
United States				
To mind	13.4	15.8	23.5	16.7
To be independent	26.1	26.3	18.3	25.0
n	134	38	213	12

Figure 1. Theoretical Model: The Value of Children and Childrearing Patterns

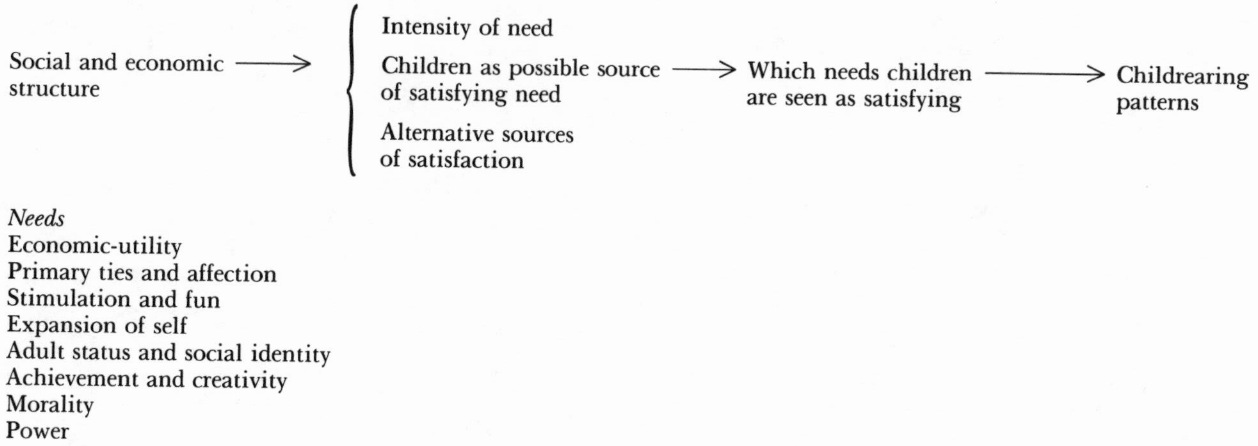

Social and economic ⟶ { Intensity of need ⟶ Which needs children ⟶ Childrearing
structure   Children as possible source   are seen as satisfying   patterns
                          of satisfying need

                          Alternative sources
                          of satisfaction

Needs
Economic-utility
Primary ties and affection
Stimulation and fun
Expansion of self
Adult status and social identity
Achievement and creativity
Morality
Power

A number of papers have come out of the cross-national study showing how the socioeconomic structure influences which needs children satisfy (Hoffman and Manis, 1979; Hoffman, Thornton, and Manis, 1978). We will focus here on three of the needs: economic-utility, primary ties and affection, and achievement and creativity, examining the relationship between these needs and childrearing goals.

Needs Children Satisfy

There were many different approaches, in the Cross-National Value of Children study, to measuring the major variable: What are the needs that children satisfy for parents? The primary measure was based on responses to the following question: "I want to ask you about the advantages and disadvantages of having children. First, what would you say are some of the advantages or good things about having children compared with not having children at all?"

Because this was the first question, it was unaffected by any other question in the interview. It was a completely open question and yielded rich responses. The answers were coded according to a highly specific and differentiated coding scheme. Sixty-five different types of responses were coded, with a maximum of four per person. The coding scheme was in large part empirical, adapted for the particular responses, but it was guided by and organized around the eight categories listed in Figure 1 that represent basic psychological needs. Thus, while the specific satisfactions of parenthood grouped together under each of the eight categories might be very different in form, they all satisfy the same basic psychological need.

Table 4 shows the percentage of mothers who indicated that children satisfied a particular basic need. For example, 54 percent of the Turkish mothers indicated that children satisfied an economic-utility need, while 46 percent did not include this in their answer. Since more than one answer was given, the percentages in the columns do not total 100 (Hoffman, 1987; Hoffman and Manis, 1979).

Table 4 shows that the three most common needs children satisfy are economic-utility, the need for primary ties and affection (or love), and the need for fun and stimulation. For Turkey, Indonesia, the Philippines, and Thailand, the most common value of children mentioned is economic-utility. Such answers, on the other hand, are much less frequent in the United States. Primary ties, the love response, is the most common in the United States, while stimulation and fun is the most common in Korea, Taiwan, and Singapore. Because the number of responses given and coded differs somewhat from country to country (Thailand being particularly low), it is more meaningful to compare the relative importance of the values in each country than the actual percentages of any particular response.

Table 4. Advantages of Having Children Reported by Mothers, by Country (Percentage)

	Turkey	Indonesia (Javanese)	Indonesia (Sundanese)	Philippines	Thailand	Korea	Taiwan	Singapore	United States
Economic-utility	54.0	94.1	79.6	71.3	74.6	35.7	44.4	46.8	6.0
Primary ties and affection	34.3	14.0	34.7	46.1	12.9	36.8	44.8	58.6	66.1
Stimulation and fun	21.7	12.8	38.2	58.2	9.2	46.8	68.6	70.9	60.0
Expansion of self	10.4	28.6	41.5	8.9	4.7	23.7	38.1	21.2	35.3
Adult status and social identity	13.8	2.1	4.7	5.9	2.0	5.8	8.3	9.1	21.9
Achievement	4.6	7.8	7.7	3.4	1.8	30.1	2.8	3.0	11.1
Morality	6.7	0.5	0.4	1.9	1.9	2.3	0.4	0.2	6.8
Power	1.8	0.1	0.2	2.0	0.1	1.2	0.1	0.2	2.2
n	1,539	984	965	1,567	2,288	1,433	2,103	904	1,259

Parental Goals

The Cross-National Value of Children study included two measures of parental goals. One was the question already cited that asked what qualities parents wanted in their children at school age, given a list of five. A second question asked what qualities parents wanted in their children when grown: "We are interested in the qualities and characteristics that people like to see in their children when they grow up. (If you had a son) what kind of person would you want him to become?" The same question was asked about daughters. The second set of questions were open-ended. The mothers' responses are shown in Table 5.

The Relationship Between Needs and Goals

The relationship between the needs children satisfy for parents and the parental goals for children was examined separately for three different groups: elementary school educated, high school educated, and college educated. A control on education was necessary because, in all eight countries, both the needs children satisfy and the parental goals were related to education (Hoffman, 1980); there were also substantial educational differences among the countries. In addition, the relationships between the needs and the goals, as discussed below, are different for different education groups. Since this was a complicated and expensive operation to carry out across the full set of countries, five were selected for this analysis: Turkey, Korea, Taiwan, Singapore, and the United States. Unless otherwise specified, all statistics in this section are two-tailed chi squares with one degree of freedom and are based on the mothers' responses. Questions about adult goals for children were sex-specific; except when indicated, statistics are based on the question about sons.

Economic-Utilitarian. Parents who indicated that children are wanted for economic or utilitarian reasons should be more likely to expect obedience from them and less likely to want them to be independent; that is, to rear children to be obedient would tend to increase the likelihood that the children will help their parents both as children and as adults. Indeed, as Table 6 shows, parents who gave an economic-utilitarian advantage of having children tended to indicate that the most important quality for a school-age child was to mind and were less likely to select independence. These relationships were statistically significant in Korea, Taiwan, and Turkey. They were not significant for the elementary school educated in Singapore, and the pattern did not hold in the United States where economic-utilitarian responses were less common than in the other countries and only 16 percent of the mothers chose "to mind."

Table 5. Percentage of Mothers Mentioning Qualities Desired in Sons and Daughters When Grown[a]

	Turkey		Philippines		Korea		Taiwan		Singapore		United States	
	Sons	Daughters	Sons	Daughters	Sons	Daughters	Sons	Daughters	Sons	Daughters	Sons	Daughters
Helpful to parents, utilitarian	0.0	0.0	8.1	14.4	16.9	16.3	0.0	0.0	1.3	0.0	0.0	0.0
Close and loving to parents	22.4	17.1	3.9	4.6	0.0	0.0	40.6	43.4	10.0	2.2	1.2	1.6
Obedient	0.0	0.0	25.0	23.2	0.0	0.0	0.3	0.2	21.2	5.0	0.0	0.0
Moral virtue	23.0	9.4	55.4	47.8	68.8	52.8	68.6	52.6	55.2	30.5	54.6	55.2
Family man, homemaker	12.1	36.7	1.0	2.5	1.7	19.2	2.1	18.2	0.7	0.1	4.8	13.5
Marry well	2.8	12.8	0.1	0.5	0.0	2.8	0.2	7.8	0.0	0.0	0.0	0.2
Health and appearance	3.5	4.8	2.6	4.2	7.5	12.1	2.3	4.3	0.7	0.4	6.4	4.3
Social viewpoint	0.9	0.5	0.0	0.0	6.2	3.9	0.1	0.0	0.0	0.0	0.6	0.4
Good manners	16.3	14.6	5.7	3.7	1.7	3.1	1.7	1.8	15.8	3.9	7.9	9.3
Conforming, conventional	0.0	0.0	0.2	0.2	2.6	1.4	0.0	0.1	0.4	0.4	1.2	0.9
Personable qualities	44.0	36.6	5.7	5.7	2.8	2.9	13.1	22.3	5.4	1.7	51.4	48.5
Career, job	38.5	21.3	28.2	26.4	9.7	6.1	33.5	17.1	20.2	5.5	14.3	10.0
Educated, studious, able	55.7	44.1	26.2	22.0	23.0	14.7	25.8	30.0	37.5	15.2	17.9	17.6
Hardworking, diligent	9.8	4.5	20.1	19.7	7.6	2.6	11.4	5.2	23.2	11.4	18.0	9.2
Independent, mature, strong	7.0	7.3	5.3	3.9	34.3	17.9	21.8	9.7	31.6	10.2	31.7	32.5
Self-fulfilled, actualized	0.3	0.3	0.3	0.3	3.5	2.6	0.9	1.5	0.2	0.1	2.6	2.6
Repressed, quiet, calm	0.7	0.8	1.5	9.4	16.7	42.9	1.1	0.7	0.0	0.0	3.1	2.6
Not trouble or disgrace	0.0	0.0	5.1	1.5	0.0	0.0	2.4	0.0	0.0	0.0	0.8	0.6
n	1,527	1,527	1,571	1,571	1,439	1,439	2,103	2,103	901	901	1,259	1,259

[a] Any of first three answers

This same pattern also showed up when the open-ended questions about the qualities desired in their children as adults were considered. There was a tendency for those who gave an economic-utilitarian reason for having children to fail to cite independence as a desired quality in their sons or daughters when they were grown (statistically significant in Singapore, the United States, Taiwan, except for the college educated, and among the more educated in Turkey). Obedience was not a common adult goal except in Singapore, but here the pattern was also apparent; those for whom children had a utilitarian value were most likely to indicate they wanted obedience. Table 7 shows that 30.6 percent of the mothers with no more than an elementary school education who mentioned a utilitarian reason for wanting children also said they wanted obedience in their sons when they were adult. This is in contrast to 15.1 percent of those comparably educated who did not cite the utilitarian value ($p < 0.05$). For the group with high school education, the figures were 27.4 percent in contrast with 10.4 percent ($p < 0.05$).

The utilitarian value of children is more prevalent in countries with predominantly rural economies, and, in every country in the cross-national study, rural residence was related to citing this value (Hoffman, 1980). It seems quite possible that the link between the agricultural life and the value on obedience is that in these settings children have a utilitarian value. If they are obedient, they will fill that function.

This formulation is different from LeVine's theory, but it is not inconsistent. Parents may seek obedience in their children both because it serves them and because it serves the child. We are focusing on the former when we say that rural parents value their children for utilitarian reasons and encouraging obedience maximizes the attainment of this value. LeVine, on the other hand, would say that obedience is a goal because it will help the children survive as adults. Both processes may be occurring, and in this particular example we have what Super and Harkness (1981) might consider "goodness of fit": The parents' needs and the child's needs coincide.

Parents citing the utilitarian value of children should also be likely to specify that they want their children to be helpful to their parents when grown. Although this tendency can be seen in the Korean data, the other countries did not mention this adult goal often enough to examine it ($p < 0.05$ for Korean elementary- and college-educated groups).

The possibility of maximizing the child's utilitarian value, particularly support in old age, would be enhanced in some settings by the son's having a good job, particularly where he was expected to have a job rather than to join his father in agriculture or business. The wish that the son have a good job was more often mentioned by the women with a high school education or more who also cited the utilitarian values in the United States, Taiwan, and Korea ($p < 0.05$).

Table 6. The Utility Value of Children by Quality Most Desired in Child

	Turkey						Korea					
	Mention			No Mention			Mention			No Mention		
	Ele	HS	Col	Ele	HS	Col	Ele	HS	Col	Ele	HS	Col
Mind	41.2	16.2	—	36.6	11.7	4.9	26.1	9.0	0.0	16.0	5.8	0.0
Independent	6.6	29.2	—	10.2	34.1	48.8	25.0	70.1	85.7	30.3	73.1	84.4
Popular	7.7	9.4	—	7.0	9.0	4.9	8.7	2.1	0.0	7.2	2.7	1.3
Do well in school	15.7	3.8	—	16.2	7.6	7.3	21.7	8.0	4.8	26.4	7.8	2.6
Good person	29.8	43.4	—	30.0	35.7	34.2	17.4	10.7	9.5	20.1	10.7	11.7
n	739	53	8	727	157	41	353	187	21	512	413	77

	Taiwan						Singapore					
	Mention			No Mention			Mention			No Mention		
	Ele	HS	Col	Ele	HS	Col	Ele	HS	Col	Ele	HS	Col
Mind	27.9	11.3	25.0	21.8	7.6	7.1	32.5	34.5	—	30.0	18.2	—
Independent	15.1	35.7	37.5	16.5	44.7	42.9	34.7	34.5	—	35.7	51.0	—
Popular	9.0	7.8	6.3	7.3	6.8	14.3	1.1	1.2	—	2.0	2.7	—
Do well in school	10.0	20.0	18.8	15.6	18.1	23.8	10.0	15.5	—	8.4	7.7	—
Good person	38.0	25.12	12.5	38.9	22.8	11.9	21.6	14.3	—	24.0	20.5	—
n	836	115	16	970	237	42	361	84	1	297	220	5

United States

	Mention			No Mention		
	Ele	*HS*	*Col*	*Ele*	*HS*	*Col*
Mind	—	11.3	10.7	17.7	19.9	7.7
Independent	—	22.5	25.0	23.5	21.3	33.1
Popular	—	9.9	7.1	0.0	2.6	1.2
Do well in school	—	14.1	7.1	23.5	11.4	5.2
Good person	—	42.3	50.0	35.3	44.8	58.8
n	1	71	28	17	957	483

Table 7. The Utility Value of Children by Adult Qualities Desired in Sons (Percentage)

	Turkey						Korea					
	Mention			No Mention			Mention			No Mention		
	Ele	HS	Col	Ele	HS	Col	Ele	HS	Col	Ele	HS	Col
Helpful to parents	0.0	0.0	0.0	0.0	0.0	0.0	26.1	11.8	14.3	19.5	10.0	1.5
Obedience	0.0	0.0	0.0	0.0	0.0	0.0	0.0	0.0	0.0	0.0	0.0	0.0
Independence	6.0	11.3	2.5	5.5	13.3	24.4	29.8	40.1	42.9	30.1	40.9	41.6
Job	40.3	22.6	62.5	39.2	28.5	19.5	7.1	11.2	14.3	9.8	10.7	3.9
Education	54.1	49.1	37.5	60.1	52.0	46.3	31.7	19.3	9.5	24.6	14.5	22.1
n	740	53	8	730	158	41	353	187	21	512	413	77

	Taiwan						Singapore					
	Mention			No Mention			Mention			No Mention		
	Ele	HS	Col	Ele	HS	Col	Ele	HS	Col	Ele	HS	Col
Helpful to parents	0.0	0.0	0.0	0.0	0.0	0.0	2.7	2.4	—	0.3	0.0	—
Obedience	0.0	0.9	0.0	0.5	0.4	0.0	30.6	27.4	—	15.1	10.4	—
Independence	12.1	27.8	43.8	17.6	35.4	35.7	27.1	29.8	—	33.6	37.4	—
Job	36.2	38.3	43.8	32.9	24.5	16.7	19.7	20.4	—	21.5	20.1	—
Education	21.9	12.0	25.0	28.8	27.9	23.8	41.0	54.8	—	27.7	38.7	—
n	836	115	16	971	237	42	366	84	—	298	222	5

United States

	Mention			No Mention		
	Ele	HS	Col	Ele	HS	Col
Helpful to parents	—	0.0	0.0	0.0	0.0	0.0
Obedience	—	0.0	0.0	0.0	0.0	0.0
Independence	—	15.5	39.3	5.9	28.2	45.3
Job	—	23.9	10.7	29.4	15.2	8.9
Education	—	26.8	39.3	11.8	17.2	22.4
n	1	71	28	17	959	483

Education, however, is a complicated goal in relation to the utilitarian need. On the one hand, it may be the path to upward mobility so that the educated child would be in a better position to help his or her parents. On the other hand, it is sometimes seen as a route by which parents lose control over their children and cannot count on their support. In the most urban of the five countries being examined here, the United States and Singapore, educational goals are significantly ($p < 0.05$) more often cited by respondents who mentioned the utilitarian value, but this relationship is not observed in the other three countries.

Parents who mention utilitarian advantages do in fact expect more help from their children in each of the various countries (Hoffman and Manis, 1979; Bulatao, 1979), and data from the Cross-National Value of Children study, as well as from previous research, indicate that, when the needed help is best provided by one sex, usually the male, there is a preference for that sex. In the Value of Children study, this pattern was particularly strong in Korea, Taiwan, and Turkey, and respondents specifically indicated that one reason for preferring sons was their greater potential for economic contributions. In the Philippines, on the other hand, daughters are valued for their help in the household and fields as children, and so, while the economic-utility value is high here, sex preference is not (Arnold, Chung, and Kuo, 1982; Bulatao, 1981).

Primary Ties and Affection. The most common component of the responses indicating that children help satisfy the need for love and primary ties was that children bring love and provide companionship. A second component frequently cited was that they strengthen the marriage. For example, respondents who indicated that children bring love and companionship should want loving and companionable children. One group of responses given to the question about the qualities desired in sons and daughters when grown seems particularly appropriate. This is a group called personal qualities that included responses like "outgoing," "warm," "loving," "good-natured," "cheerful," "not boring," "good sense of humor," and "straightforward." These are qualities one might like in a friend, and it is not surprising that respondents who gave the "bring love and companionship" response were most likely to answer this question in such terms for both sons and daughters. Among the five countries used for this analysis, this pattern was most pronounced for the United States, Singapore, and Turkey. In these three countries, the pattern was apparent (significant with $p < 0.05$ or close to significant with $p < 0.10$) for each educational group. The relationship was not as clear, however, for Taiwan and Korea.

The implication of the second component—to benefit or enhance the marriage—is that the child will increase the love from the spouse and is primarily a means to this end. In all countries examined and almost all educational groups, whether the respondent was discussing sons or daughters, those who indicated this as an advantage of children were more likely also to indicate that their wish for their children was that they be independent. This relationship could not be tested for the college educated in Singapore or the elementary educated in the United States because there were too few cases. Furthermore, "to benefit the marriage" was not fully coded in Turkey (Hoffman, 1980). All other chi squares were computed and found to be statistically significant with one exception—the college-educated Taiwanese. Although this pattern was most apparent for the open-ended question about adult goals, a similar tendency existed for the fixed-response question about qualities desired in school-age children: Those who valued children for their function for the marriage were also likely to want independent children (statistically significant for the high school educated in the United States, the elementary educated in Singapore, the elementary and high school educated in Taiwan and Korea). Without a control on education and country, it would be easy to dismiss this as a spurious relationship with both the marriage focus and the child-independence goal each reflecting simply a more modern and educated view, but the pervasiveness of the relationship across the various groups suggests it is a true one. The data suggest that, when children are wanted to enhance the marriage, it is expected that they not intrude too much on the marriage; they should be independent.

Achievement, Competence, and Creativity. Valuing children because they satisfy a need for achievement or creativity can take several forms. For some men and women, particularly with no children as yet, the sheer physical creativity is a motivation for having children and a source of satisfaction after the child's birth. This was mentioned more often in the United States than in the other countries in the cross-national study. In some of the older studies, the number of children (Hoffman and Hoffman, 1973; Hoffman, 1974; Livson and Day, 1977) or the number of sons gave parents a sense of achievement. Most of the achievement needs expressed in the cross-national study, however, referred to the sense of doing a job well, and thus satisfaction was to be gained in the quality of the child. Most respondents, then, who indicated that the advantage of children was to give the parents a sense of achievement could be expected to have the goal of rearing a child with the qualities they esteem. For example, "doing well in school" was more often cited as the desired quality in school-age children by those who indicated the achievement advantage, but this was mainly true for educated respondents. In the United States, among the college educated, twice as many of the mothers who mentioned the achievement advantage also chose school performance ($p < 0.05$).

A more pervasive pattern in the Cross-National Value of Children study was an association between citing the achievement advantage and choosing as the adult goals for sons and daughters qualities we have called "virtue." These include "a good person," "an honest person," "a decent person who doesn't fight or drink," "God-fearing man," "someone kind and loving," "one who respects others." This category of goals was more often mentioned for both sons and daughters by persons who also indicated the achievement advantage in the United States, Singapore, Turkey, and Taiwan, and for daughters in Korea. In the five countries examined here, the only exception to this relationship was in Korea where citing the achievement advantage went with choosing education ($p < 0.05$, elementary school; $p < 0.10$, high school) and hard work ($p < 0.05$, college; $p < 0.10$, elementary school) as the adult goals for sons, rather than what we have labeled "virtue."

Conclusion

This chapter has reviewed some of the theories of cultural differences in childrearing patterns and proposed a new theory which holds that children satisfy certain needs for parents and the specific needs they satisfy affects the parents' childrearing orientations. This theory is part of a more general one, elaborated and investigated in previous publications (Hoffman and Hoffman, 1973; Hoffman, Thornton, and Manis, 1978; Hoffman and Manis, 1979), that views the value of children to parents as embedded in an interaction between basic psychological needs and social structure. In exploring this new theory, we have discussed some tentative conclusions: Respondents who saw children as satisfying economic-utility needs were more likely to want obedient than independent children, and, among the more educated, there was also a wish for sons to have "good jobs" as adults. Respondents who valued children as a source of love and companionship sought qualities of congeniality in their children, while those who saw children as strengthening the marital relationship wanted independent children. Among the educated respondents, those who sought achievement satisfaction in children wanted their children to do well in school, but most respondents who sought achievement satisfaction from parenthood set moral virtue as their goal for children.

The only control variables used in this discussion were the country, education, and sex of the respondent. An actual test of the hypotheses would require a much more complex data analysis and a full array of measures of childrearing patterns. Nevertheless, the data have been useful in supporting the viability of the theory and in suggesting hypotheses and approaches for further research.

No attempt has been made to assert the superior validity of any one theory. There are many different factors that affect parenting attitudes and behavior. Some patterns develop that maximize the child's chances for survival; these may be similar across the species or different as environmental conditions are different. Some patterns may reflect the values of the parents that are derived from their occupational pursuits or may be geared to fit the child for his or her expected adult roles. Some patterns of childrearing may reflect cultural beliefs even where their etiology is not clear. But some patterns also may develop out of the needs of parents that children might fulfill. The theories are not incompatible; they simply focus on different, interacting processes.

References

Arnold, F., Chung, B. J., and Kuo, E. *Boy or Girl: A Comparative Study of Gender Preference of Parents*. Unpublished manuscript, Honolulu, Hawaii: East-West Population Institute, 1982.

Barry, H., III, Bacon, M. K., and Child, I. L. "Definitions, Ratings, and Bibliographic Sources for Child-Training Practices of 110 Cultures." In C. S. Ford (ed.), *Cross-Cultural Approaches*. New Haven, Conn.: HRAF Press, 1967.

Barry, H., III, Child, I. L., and Bacon, M. K. "Relation of Child Training to Subsistence Economy." *American Anthropologist*, 1959, *61*, 51–63.

Bulatao, R. A. *On the Nature of the Transition in the Value of Children*. Paper no. 60-A. Honolulu, Hawaii: East-West Population Institute, 1979.

Bulatao, R. A. *Roots of the Preference for Sons or Daughters: Comparisons of Husbands and Wives in Seven Countries*. Unpublished manuscript, Honolulu, Hawaii: East-West Population Institute, 1981.

Hoffman, L. W. "The Employment of Women, Education, and Fertility." *Merrill Palmer Quarterly*, 1974, *20* (2), 99–119.

Hoffman, L. W. "Changes in Family Roles, Socialization, and Sex Differences." *American Psychologist*, 1977, *32*, 644–657.

Hoffman, L. W. "Assessment of the Adequacy of Measures and Theory in a Cross-Cultural Investigation of the Value of Children to Parents." Paper presented at a meeting of the International Congress of Psychology, Leipzig, German Democratic Republic, July 1980.

Hoffman, L. W. "Work, Family, and the Socialization of the Child." In R. D. Parke (ed.), *The Family: Review of Child Development Research*. Vol. 7. Chicago: University of Chicago Press, 1984.

Hoffman, L. W. "Work, Family, and the Child." In M. S. Pallak and R. O. Perloff (eds.), *Psychology and Work: Productivity, Change, and Employment*. Washington, D.C.: American Psychological Association, 1986.

Hoffman, L. W. "The Value of Children to Parents and Childrearing Patterns." *Social Behavior*, 1987, *2*, 123–141.

Hoffman, L. W., and Hoffman, M. L. "The Value of Children to Parents." In J. T. Fawcett (ed.), *Psychological Perspectives on Fertility*. New York: Basic Books, 1973.

Hoffman, L. W., and Manis, J. D. "The Value of Children in the United States: A New Approach to the Study of Fertility." *Marriage and the Family*, 1979, *42*, 583–596.

Hoffman, L. W., Thornton, A., and Manis, J. D. "The Value of Children to Parents in the United States." *Population, Behavioral, Social, and Environmental Issues*, 1978, *1*, 91–131.

Kohn, M. L. "Social Class and Parent-Child Relationships: An Interpretation." *American Journal of Sociology*, 1963, *68*, 471–480.

122

Kohn, M. L. *Class and Conformity: A Study in Values.* Homewood, Ill.: Dorsey Press, 1969.

Kohn, M. L. *Personlichkeit, Beruf, und Soziale Schichtung: Ein Bezugsrahmen [Personality, Occupation, and Social Situation: A Frame of Reference].* Heidelberg, West Germany: Klett-Cotta, 1980.

Langman, L. "Economic Practices and Socialization in Three Societies." Paper presented at the meeting of the American Sociological Association, New York, August 1973.

LeVine, R. A. "Parental Goals: A Cross-Cultural View." *Teachers College Record,* 1974, *76* (2), 226–239.

Livson, N., and Day, D. "Adolescent Personality Antecedents of Completed Family Size: A Longitudinal Study." *Journal of Youth and Adolescence,* 1977, *6,* 311–324.

Munroe, R. H., and Munroe, R. L. "Obedience Among Children in an East African Society." *Journal of Cross-Cultural Psychology,* 1972, *3,* 395–399.

Poffenberger, T., and Poffenberger, S. B. "The Social Psychology of Fertility Behavior in a Village in India." In J. Fawcett (ed.), *Psychological Perspectives on Population.* New York: Basic Books, 1973.

Super, C. M., and Harkness, S. "Figure, Ground, and Gestalt: The Cultural Context of the Active Individual." In R. M. Lerner and N. A. Busch-Rossnagel (eds.), *Individuals as Producers of Their Development: A Life-Span Perspective.* New York: Academic Press, 1981.

Super, C. M., and Harkness, S. "The Development of Affect in Infancy and Early Children." In D. A. Wagner and H. W. Stevenson (eds.), *Cultural Perspectives on Child Development.* San Francisco: W. H. Freeman, 1982.

United Nations. *Statistical Yearbook.* (33d ed.). New York: United Nations, 1982.

Lois Wladis Hoffman is professor of psychology and chair of the developmental area at the University of Michigan.

Index

A

"Accident Mortality at the Preschool Ages," 69, 73
Adaptive behavior: in Kenya, 30, 32; in Yucatán, 10
Agrarian parental strategies, 6-7, 8, 9, 10, 11; in Fiji Islands, 13-25; in Kenya, 27-35; in Yucatán, 37-50
Altmann, J., 6, 11
Ambrose, J. A., 41, 49
American Anthropological Association, 1
American Scandinavian Foundation, 75
Arnold, F., 100, 118, 121

B

Bacon, M. K., 99, 100, 121
Bakeman, R., 87, 96
Ban, P., 82, 85, 96
Barlow, K., 21, 24
Barry, H., III, 99, 100, 121
Bass, J., 69, 73
Bayley Mental Development Index, 31
Becker, A., 17, 24
Behavior of Fiji parents, 13-25
Behavior of Kenya parents: and birth ceremonies in Kenya, 33; and bottle-feeding, 32; and breast-feeding, 33; changes in, 32-34; and education, 33-34
Behavior of parents, based on goals, 4-6
Behavioral profiles, in five-culture study, 90-95
Benigni, L., 53, 55, 61, 62
Birth intervals, 10; in Fiji Islands, 18, 19-20; in Kenya, 7, 29-30; in United States, 67; in Yucatán, 42-44, 45-46
Boston. See United States
Bottle-feeding: and illness in Yucatán, 45-47; in Kenya, 32; for social status in Yucatán, 47; as survival

consideration in Yucatán, 47; versus breast-feeding in Yucatán, 45-49
Bowlby, J., 3, 11
Brackbill, Y., 41, 49
Brazelton Neonatal Behavioral Assessment Scale, 31
Brazelton, T. B., 30-31, 34, 72, 73
Breast-feeding, 7, 10, 30; attitudes on, in Sweden, 78; in Kenya, 33; and lack of illness in Yucatán, 45-47; versus bottle-feeding in Yucatán, 45-49; in Yucatán, 43
Brittenham, G., 60, 62
Brown, J. K., 20, 24
Bulatao, R. A., 100, 118, 121
Buripakdi, C., 100

C

Caldwell, J., 4, 11
Callaghan, J., 82, 96
Caregivers, 66; categories of, in Yucatán, 44-45; fathers as, in Sweden, 77, 78-79; in Fiji Islands, 21-23; in Italy, 58-60; in Kenya, 32; in Sweden, 79; in Yucatán, 41-42
Caron, J., 31, 34
Carrier, A. H., 21, 24
Carroll, V., 23, 24
Catrine, class division in Yucatán, 40
Caudill, W., 3, 4, 11, 69, 73
Child, I. L., 99, 100, 121
Childrearing patterns: in different cultures, 102-109; model of, 108
Chisholm, J., 56, 62, 82, 96
Chung, B. J., 100, 118, 121
Cipolla, C., 53, 62
Civita Fantera. See Italy
Class divisions, in Yucatán, 40
Communication with infants. See Verbal interaction; Visual interaction
Comparative Human Infancy Project, 1
Containers, for U.S. infants, 67, 69-70